PEOPLE WHO RUN EUROPE

People Who Run Europe

EDWARD C. PAGE

CLARENDON PRESS · OXFORD
1997

Oxford University Press, Great Clarendon Street, Oxford OX2 6DP
Oxford New York
Athens Auckland Bangkok Bogota Bombay
Buenos Aires Calcutta Cape Town Dar es Salaam Delhi
Florence Hong Kong Istanbul Karachi
Kuala Lumpur Madras Madrid Melbourne
Mexico City Nairobi Paris Singapore
Taipei Tokyo Toronto
and associated companies in
Berlin Ibadan

Oxford is a trade mark of Oxford University Press

Published in the United States
by Oxford University Press Inc., New York

British Library Cataloguing in Publication Data
Data available

Library of Congress Cataloging in Publication Data
Page, Edward.
People who run Europe / Edward C. Page.
Includes bibliographical references.
1. European Union—Officials and employees. I. Title.
JN35.P34 1996 354.1'0422—dc20 96–32409
ISBN 0–19–828079–3

1 3 5 7 9 10 8 6 4 2

Typeset by Graphicraft Typesetters Ltd., Hong Kong
Printed in Great Britain
on acid-free paper by
Biddles Ltd, Guildford and King's Lynn

ACKNOWLEDGEMENTS

This book is a product of Economic and Social Research Council Grant FR000233768. Linda Wouters worked with me on this project and gave assistance above and beyond the call of duty. Ms Wouters compiled the data on which the study is based. I am grateful to the EU officials who generously helped by providing documents, information, and opinion about life within the EU civil service. Ms June Burnham, Mr Dionyssis Dimitrakopoulos, Professor Morten Egeberg, Professor Michael Goldsmith, Mr Thomas Hailer, Professor Jack Hayward, Professor George Jones, and Mr Rüdiger Wurzel have offered useful critical comments on drafts of this book. I am grateful to all of these people.

CONTENTS

LIST OF FIGURES

LIST OF TABLES

1

Bureaucracy and the European Union

1. INTRODUCTION

Bureaucracy and the European Union are easily associated. For many sceptical about closer European integration, whether they are in Britain, Norway, France, Germany, or anywhere else, one of the main problems of the European Union is that it is a remote bureaucracy pursuing standardization and making the everyday life of its 380 million citizens fit the Procrustean bed designed in Brussels (European Commission 1994*a*). The European Union's organizations bear names reminiscent of the dull bureaucratized life of Orwell's 1984—Europol or DG XXIII. The people who head them hold aloof titles such as Commissioner or Director General. The laws are known by abstract numbers instead of simple names—Directive 78/319 on waste management. The impetus behind these laws is not a party manifesto nor public clamour over a pressing issue, but comes from discussions largely conducted by officials in Brussels. Politics in Brussels is conducted in the language of bureaucratic obfuscation; disagreements are handled by 'clarifications' rather than any one side of the argument winning or losing. Words such as 'federalism' are said to have flatly different meanings in different languages and cultures; new words such as 'subsidiarity' are introduced into the language in order to soothe any who are troubled by more traditional words such as 'sovereignty'.

This view of the sceptic finds at least some echo with the supporter of closer European integration. Even the German Federal Chancellor, Helmut Kohl, has managed to combine a strong commitment to an ever closer union with criticism of bureaucratic interference from Brussels. For Kohl, overzealous administration risked the European Union 'squandering its authority on petty interference' and could thus diminish its ability to 'drive forward the grand European project' (MacIntyre and Helm 1995). More generally, in the 1980s and 1990s increasing attention has been paid to the problem of the 'democratic deficit' within the European Union. Although the Council, a body composed of the elected governments of member states, is the main decision-making body in the EU, other publicly elected representatives are insufficiently involved in the process. The reason for this lack of involvement is not a Brussels bureaucracy bent on keeping power for itself, but rather the reluctance of political leaders within many member states to hand over power to democratically elected representatives in Europe. Nevertheless it is a serious problem, and one that could be addressed by measures such as a stronger institutionalization of legislative control and scrutiny of European legislation and administrative activity within the parliamentary structures of member states (Brittan 1994) or, more simply, greater powers to the European Parliament (Lodge 1985).

There can be little doubt that the European Union at least throws into sharper relief that which is invariably true in the national governments of its member states, the general principle that unelected civil servants are powerful. While observers such as Putnam (1973) have suggested that bureaucracies were dominated for much of this century by 'classical' bureaucrats—those who simply obeyed orders and eschewed any involvement in policy-making—there is little evidence to support this view (see Page 1992). Moreover, such 'classical' officials would be of little use to their political masters. Civil servants everywhere not only have the opportunity as permanent officials with expertise in decision-making to shape the decisions they are also responsible for implementing—they are expected to shape them. Yet the constitution of the European Union, as set out in the Treaty of Rome and last amended in the Maastricht Treaty, goes somewhat further and explicitly gives powers to the Commission that are not given to unelected bodies elsewhere, such as the power to call meetings of the key legislative body of the Union, the Council of Ministers, and the power to initiate legislation.

The powers of the Commission make the question of the role of bureaucracy in the European Union pressing. In addition, the day-to-day process of decision-making places civil servants, European and national, in a potentially powerful position. The bulk of the linkages between member states and the European Union are conducted through permanent officials, whether regional, national, or European, not through ministers or parliamentarians. On top of the official permanent representations of member states in Brussels (see Hayes-Renshaw *et al.* 1989), there are large numbers of officials based in their home states who regularly participate in groups. Some of these groups are formally constituted, such as the *comitologie* committees (which have to be consulted on Commission legislation) or the host of advisory and consultative committees, while others are informal. Officials from member states may in this way seek to shape public policy and facilitate its passage through an unusually complicated patchwork of institutional relationships and thus can give expression to an even more intricate set of geographical and functional interests. Moreover, one might also argue that the nature of the policy issues with which the EU deals tend to give a greater role in decision-making to those with technical expertise—a group which would include bureaucrats. Thus Peterson (1995) suggests one of the most important distinctive characteristics of the European Union is the importance to EU policy-making of technical issues and technocratic, non-political, actors.

When faced with this apparently large role for bureaucrats in the European Union it might at first seem reasonable to ask the question: 'who governs—politicians or bureaucrats?' Such a simple question is unanswerable. We have no means of measuring the relative power of the politicians of the European Parliament and the Council of Ministers, and moreover no way of determining whether bureaucrats themselves might be acting on behalf of politicians, or in anticipation of their reactions. The literature on decision-making in the European Union suggests that no simple consistent answer can be given to such a question. The balance of power as between the array of institutions, groups, and nations, as reflected in having a decisive impact on European legislation, changes from issue to issue and time to time; under a forceful commissioner the power within a Directorate General might lie with the commissioner and his or her[1] *cabinet*, while a predecessor might have left much to be decided by a Director or Director General; under the presidency of one country, advice for policy initiatives might be sought more actively from groups outside the EU—consultants or interest groups—while under the presidency of another greater reliance is placed upon the Commission as a source of initiative; some conflicts can be settled only after bilateral ministerial agreements between large member states, while others can be ironed out through multilateral deals struck by domestic and European civil servants. In the decision-making structure of the European Union it is very difficult to talk of

[1] I use 'his or her' for the commissioner and the senior officials within the European Union even though the holders of these posts have been overwhelmingly male. Since its origins in 1957 as the High Commission of the ECSC up until the Santer Commission of 1995 the College of Commissioners had only ever had two women members. There are five women in the current Santer Commission. I hope that use of 'his or her' and similar conventions will not create a misleading impression of gender equality in these positions.

any one body, group, or individual holding power, if the term power refers to a long-term capacity to determine what laws the EU should pass or on what EU money should be spent. Moreover among the major actors involved in policy-making in the EU there are rarely any outright losers —accepting defeat on one issue might help secure victory on another. For example, losing a battle to get one's own nominee into a key position, often brings with it the recognition that one has a much stronger claim to decide who fills the next vacancy.

2. VISIONS OF EUROPEAN BUREAUCRACY

2a. The EU administration as a dynamic core of Europe

So what is the European Union bureaucracy really like? A variety of models may be used to analyse the role of the bureaucracy in the European Union. These models are not necessarily alternatives, but tend to stress the importance of different features of the EU administration. The original Monnet view of the European bureaucracy was it was going to be something unique. Jean Monnet, whose skill and dedication to European integration were a *sine qua non* to the development of the project, had extensive experience of the birth of important administrative organizations; he became deputy Secretary General of the League of Nations in 1919 (at the age of 30) and in 1946 he became Commissaire Général du Plan—the head of the French economic planning commissariat. While he had 'not made plans for a large-scale and lasting establishment' (Monnet 1978: 372), Monnet's vision of the bureaucracy of the High Authority of the European Coal and Steel Community, the forerunner of the European Union set up under the Schuman Treaty of 1951, was of a form of bureaucracy he had pioneered in the Commissariat du Plan. Its role was not the conventional one of devising and implementing policy. Rather it

> ought to remain a nucleus and confine itself to organizing and stimulating the work of others. For the rest, it could rely on the national civil services . . . The French Modernization Plan had proved that authority could be best exercised by small teams . . . A few hundred European civil servants would be enough to set thousands of national experts to work, and to make the powerful machinery of firms and Governments serve the aims of the Treaty. It was on this model, at least, that I was going to try to frame the first Community institutions (Monnet 1978: 373).

He envisaged European administration as a small body of officials from different backgrounds who would work together to produce solutions to common problems.

The logic behind this model in the Commissariat du Plan was to maximize the chances of survival and influence in a world of entrenched bureaucratic interests. Monnet sought to keep the Commissariat small so that 'none of its big brother ministries . . . considered it a threat worth clobbering' (Cohen 1977: 29). Cohen continues:

> The size of the Planning Commission is an important element in a definition of the relationship of the plan to the ministries. Its permanent staff of forty planners necessitates the participation of the ministries in every phase of planning: its lightweight and open structure assures that their traditional areas of competence will be respected and the fact that some of the Planning Commission's experts are merely on loan from their original departments provide additional security to the ministries

Monnet's own vision of a European administration arose from an intention to create an institution very similar to that of the Planning Commission in its ability to innovate and to adapt to the existing bureaucratic-institutional environment. The basic principle could be characterized as a the quest for creating a lean, dynamic, cosmopolitan administrative core of Europe—'human and informal' (Monnet 1978: 241). He wrote approvingly that

> there were never more than thirty senior officials on the Planning Commissariat, and the whole staff, including secretaries and doormen, was no more than a hundred or so. My own working team was smaller still—just four or five people who were with me all the time . . . But I had asked for large rooms, because I intended to bring together there the many people whose expertise we needed, but whom we did not want to add to our small permanent staff (Monnet 1978: 241).

In the European context he argued 'If one day there are more than two hundred of us, we shall have failed' (Monnet 1978: 405).

To some extent one can recognize aspects of this dynamic core of Europe model in aspects of the contemporary EU bureaucracy; European Union officials rely upon national bureaucracies to implement most European legislation. *Comitologie*, secondment (the principle of bringing in national civil servants for a short period of service in the EU administration), the system of 'parachuting' in experts from diverse backgrounds to senior positions within the bureaucracy, the extensive use of specialists under contract, as well as the diversity of backgrounds and experience of top officials and politicians within the European Union, suggest a greater fluidity in the bureaucracy, a receptiveness to a wide variety of forms of expertise and a greater willingness to draw on the experiences of other administrative organizations and promote its own interests in them than one would expect to find in a member state bureaucracy.

2b. The EU administration as an international bureaucracy

However innovative Monnet hoped the administration of the European Coal and Steel Community would be, it never conformed closely to his original ideas; even at its inception in 1952 the ECSC had far more than 200 officials and at the end of the first year of its operation it had over 550 full-time employees (see Chapter 2). Their status and conditions were certainly not novel; they were international civil servants and as such were a type of official which had developed since the early nineteenth century (Kunz 1947). Two important models for the construction of the official apparatus of the ECSC were the League of Nations Secretariat and the Secretariat of the United Nations (for a discussion of the experience of the International Secretariat of the League of Nations see Ranshofen-Wertheimer 1945). Claude, writing shortly after the initiation of the European Coal and Steel Community, suggests that the ECSC was not 'a real breakthrough in the field of international organization' (Claude 1956: 102).

The High Authority of the Coal and Steel Community incorporated many of the established features of an international civil service, including standard immunities and privileges such as inviolability of property, and immunity from some forms of taxation and certain types of prosecution (ECSC Treaty 1951, see especially 'Protocol on the Privileges and Immunities of the Community'). The contemporary administration of the European Union retains many of the original privileges and immunities which are widespread throughout many international organizations. Moreover, although it seeks genuine supranationality in the way it operates, it retains the classical problems of international bureaucracies as outlined by Inis Claude (1956: ch. 10): the 'problem of efficient administration' (reconciling the need for some 'fair representation' of nationalities within the bureaucracy with the need to have the best candidate for any job within it); the 'problem of allegiance' (securing the right balance between allegiance to the supranational authority and identification with the official's home state);

and the 'problem of political initiative' (the degree to which international officials become international statesmen).

2c. The EU administration as a typical continental bureaucracy

While it has a number of the features of an international bureaucracy, the EU administration also has much in common with a traditional model of the civil service of a continental European state. The essence of a continental European bureaucracy was in its creation of a distinctive social class that was insulated from any financial pressures which could compromise its loyalty through a generous set of pay and conditions (Hintze 1964*a*; Hood and Peters 1994). Correspondingly the continental bureaucrat enjoyed at least until the middle of this century a degree of status and financial privilege that was never entirely matched in Britain. In many ways the civil service of the European Coal and Steel Community and later the European Economic Community, European Community, and European Union shared the need for an administrative arm insulated from the pressures of an outside world. A civil service had to be created that avoided the dependence of officials on support and goodwill from their home state if European institutions were to develop any supranational European political life. Not only were its officials instructed neither to seek nor to receive instructions from their home state, after 1976 they were given an income that was both generous and secure (see Page and Wouters 1994*b*).

A number of other features of the European Union gave it the characteristics of a continental bureaucracy. The terminology of organization is generally similar to that of the French; the organizational divisions of the European Union, the *directions générales* and *directions*, and *sous-directions* mirror those of French ministerial organization as does the institution of the *cabinet*, the body of advisers and aides surrounding the commissioner, although similar terms and institutions are widespread throughout the southern part of Europe, at least partly because of French influence. There are the *concours*, or competitive entry examinations, to enter the European Union service similar to those that have been a feature of the French recruitment of civil servants for over a century. Also the ABCD grading of civil servants, introduced across the whole French civil service in 1948, as well as the ranks (*conseiller*, *directeur*, *chef de cabinet*) of officials are strongly reminiscent of French practice. Cassese (1987: 13) describes the 'organization and working rules' of the Commission as 'half way between a French ministry and the German Economics Ministry'.

Traditional continental European bureaucracies are associated with formalism and hierarchy—the insistence that rules and procedures be observed, including the political neutrality of the 'classical' bureaucrat believed by some to dominate national bureaucracies until at least the 1960s (Putnam 1973). As one disgruntled Dutch official put it

> We live under a 19th century French administrative system. A rapporteur reports to a deputy head of department, who reports to the head of department, who reports to the director, who reports to a deputy director-general, who reports to an assistant of the director-general, who reports to the director-general, who talks to the commission cabinet, which finally talks to the commissioner himself (*Guardian*, 30 July 1993).

Thus we might expect the civil servants of the European Union to have some resemblance to the type of obedient, rule-bound official associated with Max Weber's ideal type (Weber 1972).

2d. The EU administration as a subgovernmental bureaucracy

There are many points of similarity between the EU administration and an administrative system which has never had any direct influence on the development of the EU: the United States bureaucracy. As Rose points out, the US system is characterized by the absence of a focus of governmental authority—it has a subgovernment but no government (Rose 1980). Power in Washington is dispersed between legislative, executive, and judicial branches, and this separation of powers makes impossible any consistent assertion of the kind of authority asserted by cabinets or councils of ministers within Europe (for a discussion of the separation of powers in the EU context see Lenaerts 1991). Consequently, policy-making is a matter of negotiation among interest groups, congressional committees and subcommittees, and executive agencies. Whether as iron triangles, issue networks, or policy networks (Jordan 1981), the characteristic feature of such patterns of policy-making is the absence of a single locus of authority.

There are strong similarities between the fluid patterns of relationships between interest groups, executive organizations, and legislative committees and subcommittees of the type characterized by Heclo (1978) and the fluid multi-level bargaining that can be found in broad descriptions of EU policy-making such as Kassim's (1994: 22–3)

The EU's institutional density means that there are multiple points at which intra- and inter-institutional interaction takes place. With respect to intra-institutional negotiation, bargaining within the Commission may take place within the relevant unit, within the Directorate General, between the services and the Commissioner and his or her *cabinet*, between Directorate Generals, and between Commissioners within the College. Intra-institutional bargaining also takes place in intergovernmental negotiation in the Council of Ministers. Inter-institutional interaction takes place between the Commission, the Council and the European Parliament.

While Sbragia (1992) correctly warns us against looking for too close similarities between the US federal system and the emerging federation of the European Union, Peters (1992: 91) argues that the 'predictable outcome' of the organizational divisions of the European Parliament, the Council of Ministers, and the Commission is 'policy segmentation . . . much as in the United States'. The 'sectoral' model of policy-making based upon the American model has become well established in the study of policy-making in the European Union (see Mazey and Richardson 1993; Peterson 1995).

3. UNDERSTANDING BUREAUCRATIC CHARACTER

There are many familiar features of the EU administration, yet some aspects of its organization and functioning are novel. One can see reflected in it some characteristics of Monnet's vision of a new and distinctive administrative organization, but one can also catch the reflection of an international bureaucracy, as well as German, French, or even American patterns of administration. The provenance or institutional structure of the European Union administration does not give us any direct clues as to the character of its administration. What is meant by the character of the civil service? For the most part, studies which give an overall impression of the way in which civil services affect policy-making have not generated any rigorous definition of the dimensions of character, and they have been none the worse for that. They have tended to emphasize one distinctive aspect and base much of their description on that. Hugh Heclo's (1977) *Government of Strangers* in the United States emphasizes the fact that top civil servants and political appointees do not know each other and cannot be said to be part of a coherent governing élite. With Aaron Wildavsky, Heclo (Heclo and Wildavsky 1981) argues almost the opposite case in Britain where the higher levels of the civil service are characterized as a 'village community' where top officials not only know each other but have developed a distinctive set of norms and *mores*. Anton (1980) emphasizes the 'consensual' style of Swedish policy-making, Eldersveld, Kooiman, and van der Tak (1981) the importance of 'consociationalism' in the Dutch bureaucratic élite, and studies of the French civil service, most notably the works of Suleiman (1987) and Thoenig (1973), show the importance of techno-bureaucratic training and the career patterns related to it as a major key to understanding the relationship between civil service and politics. The best studies of the character of a civil service appear to be primarily inductive. Where they seek to be deductive, as in Jordan and Richardson's attempt to derive a framework of 'policy styles', they are far less informative (see Richardson 1982; Kjellberg 1984). Nevertheless, it is possible to extract some key themes from such studies of character of the civil services of nation states. These themes not only tend to feature in diverse analyses of different countries but also have strong and direct implications for the ways in which civil services affect decision-making processes.

3a. Cohesion

Perhaps the most commonly discussed characteristic of bureaucracies in single-country studies is the cohesion of the senior levels of the administration. The cohesion of the 'village community' of Heclo and Wildavsky's (1981) study of Britain contrasts with the isolated 'issue networks' Heclo (1978) identifies in the United States, as well as with the *Ressortpartikularismus* of the German civil service discussed by Mayntz and Scharpf (1975), according to which individual ministries, or even parts of individual ministries, see themselves as distinct and in competition with other ministries or parts of ministries (see also Marin and Mayntz 1991). The nature of potential divisions is also important here since the traditional departmental loyalties, which even in Britain counteract the cohesion in the higher levels of the senior civil service, are cross-cut in France by the *corps* pattern of recruitment and career development which can create both cross-ministerial cohesion and interministerial division. In the United States divisions are reinforced by the congressional committee and subcommittee system and in both Germany and the USA by the nature of the federal system which makes federal bureaucrats look outwards towards their counterparts in the states or *Länder* rather than predominantly across to their colleagues in other federal ministries or agencies.

Cohesion among top civil servants is often argued to have two main effects upon the policy process. First it is generally expected to strengthen the role of the civil service in decision-making. An internally divided body does not have the status or power of one that speaks as if with one voice. Moreover, where there are close links between officials from different ministries, interdepartmental negotiations can be conducted predominantly by bureaucrats. Hence in France the forces of cohesion in the French civil service, the Grands Corps, are one of the mainstays of civil-service power. As Suleiman (1978: 276) concludes, 'The entire elite-forming process—from initial recruitment to the mutual aid and support that members of the elite learn to give one another throughout their careers—creates a self-conscious, self-confident elite, unhampered by self-doubt' and this self-confidence is mirrored by acceptance of the status and power of the civil service among politicians and citizens alike. It is a common perception among critics of the British civil service that civil servants can arrange deals behind the backs of ministers, in gentlemen's clubs if not in the corridors of Whitehall, satirized in the popular British television comedy of the early 1980s, *Yes Minister* (Lynn and Jay 1982). One can find some evidence to support this perception in Heclo and Wildavsky's (1981: 139) study of the budgetary process where

> The minister who is not only unaggressive but also dull will be kept out of sight as much as possible. His officials will go to great lengths to settle matters with their Treasury counterparts; they will seek to make a deal, make an arrangement, accept losses they would rather not take—anything but let their feeble lamb go up to the slaughter.

Second, cohesion imparts a set of interests: since an élite is a distinctive group, it may have distinctive group interests. This observation is the basis of the whole 'bureaucratic politics' thesis which suggests that support for policy positions is influenced by institutional affiliation (see Allison 1971). There is plenty of evidence to demonstrate that different ministries or agencies within government develop distinctive ideologies (Wynia 1974), and it is a commonplace observation that civil servants in finance ministries seek to restrain spending while those in, say, social-welfare service ministries seek to increase it. Occasionally group identity and interests can extend beyond departments. The material interest of members of the French bureaucracy's Grands Corps in the fate of their particular *corps* may shape attitudes to substantive policy proposals. Thoenig (1973) argues that for decades the building of motorways in France was successfully opposed by the Ponts et Chaussées because of the feared consequences for its power base within the *départements*. Identity and interests can be service-wide as they were in France with attempts to shape the system of recruitment to the higher levels of the civil service. A service-wide group interest, according to Kellner and Crowther Hunt (1980), led the British civil service to oppose and ultimately 'defeat' many of the reform proposals set out in the 1969 Fulton Committee report (for an alternative view see Fry 1993).

3b. Institutionalized political control

A second component of the character of the bureaucracy is the form of institutionalized political control over it. Political control can be institutionalized in three main ways. First it can be institutionalized by politicizing appointments to the higher levels of the bureaucracy. The power of appointment can take the form of a politician having extensive discretion over the appointment of top officials within the bureaucracy, as in the United States where the President, at least nominally, is responsible for hundreds of top appointments in Washington.

This direct form of political appointment is not to be confused with another form of politicized appointments: 'party book administration', where membership of the correct party is a precondition for promotion to civil-service posts, with in some cases different ministries requiring different party memberships (see Dyson 1977). Given that party membership rather than personal loyalty is the major criterion for promotion, the control offered politicians by this form of linkage between politics and administration must remain questionable. This view is reinforced by the practice of officials frequently holding simultaneous membership of several parties in Austria and Belgium. Where party book administration is extensive throughout the whole national bureaucracy, and not just at its most senior levels as in Germany and to a lesser extent France, one might expect it to have the effect of reducing the political status of civil servants. The proposition that political affiliation rather than competence or even length of service is a crucial qualification for career advancement undermines the claim of civil servants to a distinctive expertise and professionalism. One would not expect this to be the case where only senior positions are subject to party book administration since length of service and professional competence are likely to have been important in advancing the careers of officials to the point where they are eligible for top jobs (see Dogan 1975: 12–16).

A second way of institutionalizing political control is through the mirror opposite to politicization: neutralization. Through insisting on the neutrality of the civil service the bureaucracy can be relied upon, in the words of Max Weber, to carry on 'working normally for the regime that comes to power after a violent revolution, for the enemy government of occupation just as it did for the legitimate governments they replace' (1972: 128). The neutrality of the civil service is a doctrine that underpins the democratic legitimacy of the civil service in Britain where Sir Donald Maitland, formerly a top civil servant, claimed (quoted in Young and Sloman 1982: 20): 'Civil servants ought not to have power because we're not elected. Power stems from the people and flows through Parliament to the minister responsible to Parliament. The civil servant has no power of his own. He is there to help a minister and to be the minister's agent.' Such a neutralization of the civil service can be found in Sweden, Norway, and Denmark, for example. Given the degree of patronage in public-sector jobs generally, it is also somewhat surprising that a similar neutralization of the top levels of the civil service is also characteristic of Italy (Hine 1993).

A third means of institutionalizing political influence is through some form of administrative body which acts as the eyes, ears, and possibly also voice of the politician within the bureaucracy. In authoritarian systems politicization takes the form of an extensive, frequently party-based, parallel administration (Caplan 1988). In European democracies such a function has been exercised to a more limited degree by the *cabinets* of ministers: a group of advisers appointed by ministers who generally have authority to act in the minister's name as well as be informed of developments within the ministry. Such *cabinet* systems are found in Belgium, France, Italy, Spain, and Portugal. The attempts by the Juppé government of 1995 to limit their size reflects a long-standing concern of French governments and is unlikely to change their importance in the politico-administrative system (Searls 1981). In a much weaker form, ministers in many other countries without formal *cabinets*, such as Britain, use advisers on an *ad hoc* basis to sustain their influence within their ministry.

All three forms of institutionalization of political control are used to some degree in most countries; civil servants, like most professional groups, generally claim some form of ability to serve others irrespective of their political views. Moreover, the impact of any single institution is not common across all countries that have adopted it. While the *cabinet* system is an essential part of the bureaucratization of politics in France, being a stepping stone from an administrative to a political career, it has no such significance and impact in Italy.

There are two broad forms of impact produced by different types of institutionalization of political control. The first can be found in the potential that such institutionalization in the form of political appointments and *cabinets* has for introducing conflict at the top of the executive organization. It is not necessarily the case that top career officials feel in competition with *cabinet* members of political appointees. Rather, career officials on the one hand and political appointees and *cabinet* members on the other have different bases of legitimacy and can have different loyalties and perceptions which may frequently conflict. In France the distinction between *cabinet* director and permanent *directeur* is a 'particularly acute conflict at the apex of the French administrative system' (Suleiman 1975: 234). Yet for the most part in France the potential conflict is substantially reduced by the fact that *cabinet* members are generally senior career civil servants.

A second consequence comes from the degree to which the institutionalization of political control creates opportunities for career officials to participate in overtly party-political decisions. All senior civil servants are involved to some degree or other in political decision-making, otherwise there would not be much interest in them. Yet the form of institutionalization of political control can encourage the development of a distinctive form of bureaucratic politician who, as a political appointee of one form or another, can advance his or her career by playing the political field. The two clearest examples are the French civil-servant politicians who pursue a career within the 'politico-administrative' élite, for which a period in a ministerial *cabinet* is a major springboard, and the American 'technopols': people who move into and out of the Washington establishment as political appointees and lobbyists. There are others: in Sweden the advisory bodies surrounding ministers create a group of bureaucratic politicians known as *politruker*. However, it cannot be assumed that any *cabinet* system creates such a group of bureaucratic politicians. In Italy the *gabbinetti* of ministers have failed to do so. The reasons for this failure are instructive: the Italian ministerial *gabbinetti* are primarily legalistic bodies, composed of a large proportion of Council of State officials, and see their role as primarily technical and not as policy-making bodies. Thus only where it has powerful decision-making powers can we expect a *cabinet* body to generate a distinctive form of bureaucratic politician.

3c. Caste or collection

The higher levels of the bureaucracy are not composed of random selections from the populations of the countries they serve. In Western nations they tend to be male, from professional backgrounds, with university degrees—the usual backgrounds for people in high-status jobs in elected politics as well as in the private sector. However, in addition to these social characteristics the higher reaches of many civil services are dominated by people with educational backgrounds that give them the appearance of a bureaucratic caste rather than simply a collection of high-status individuals. In some systems recruitment patterns create such castes. In Germany recruitment to the civil service as a *Beamte* in the top flight *höherer Dienst* is still predominantly through a *Staatsexamen* taken after studying law. Consequently, lawyers still tend to dominate in the higher levels of German administration. In France the Grandes Écoles are the training ground for senior administrators, and in Britain the universities of Oxford and Cambridge still provide nearly two-thirds of Permanent Secretaries. In other countries top administrators are a more heterogeneous collection; in Sweden the traditional dominance of legal scholars in the higher reaches of administration has given way to a great diversity of educational backgrounds.

The nature of the higher levels of the civil service as a caste has two implications for the role of the civil service in the decision-making process. The first is that a caste is more likely to be cohesive, and this in turn may be expected to affect the role of bureaucracy in the political process in the manner already outlined. Second, the nature of the caste is likely to influence the perception the bureaucratic élite has of its role in the decision-making process. A training in law on the European continent has conventionally been associated with a role perception of administration as a subordinate and largely separate world from that of politics: the 'traditional' bureaucrat of Putnam's study of Germany and Italy in the 1960s (Putnam 1973). The role perception of bureaucrats has been associated with the conception of the role of the judge in continental European Roman Law, especially in its Germanic version, as a *Paragraphenautomat*, an expert who makes no judgements but merely interprets facts in the light of existing law (see Page 1991). A different perception of role can be found among French civil servants whose training and career give them a key role in politics (Suleiman 1975: 269):

> The members of the Grands Corps . . . benefit from an aura of elitism and from a reputation for impartiality; they occupy important positions in the administrative, para-administrative and private sectors; they form part of a network within and beyond the administration, which enables them to arbitrate conflicts and coordinate policies—all of which means that they are profoundly involved in the decision making process.

In Britain the humanistic Oxford-Cambridge training that has been so characteristic of the upper reaches of the bureaucracy since the middle of the nineteenth century is passed on to new recruits since the 'civil service . . . is very proficient at moulding its bright and its young. They very quickly rub shoulders with the great, the seasoned and the established in the upper ranks and are indulged in the way that dons treat bright, sparky undergraduates who are fun to teach' (Hennessy 1989: 521). Such a training certainly does not emphasize subordination to politicians. One former permanent secretary recalled how a mentor 'showed me how to negotiate, how to draw breath mid-sentence so as to discourage interruption, how to draft, and why the service belongs neither to politicians nor to officials but to the Crown and the nation' (Sir Ian Bancroft quoted in Hennessy 1989: 521).

3d. Permeability

The permeability of civil services refers to the relationship with interest groups, and a high level of permeability is found where groups are difficult if not impossible to exclude from the policy-making process. Conversely, where interest groups are relatively easily excluded from the policy-making process the level of permeability is low. The precise influence of interest groups in policy-making varies over time and over the issue involved. Nevertheless some generalizations about the accessibility of the bureaucracy to interest groups have been possible. Some observers have examined cross-national differences under the rubric of 'non-negotiable policy making' while others have sought to use the distinction between 'strong states' and 'weak states' (Nettl 1968; Coleman 1989).

The classic case of the 'weak state' or the political system in which the scope for non-negotiable policy-making is small is the United States. In the 1970s the growth of interest organizations was one of the most profound changes affecting decision-making in Washington; large numbers of new groups, or rather groups new to Washington, transformed the existing structure of close relationships between groups and government, known as 'iron triangles', to create a series of 'issue networks' —fluid and unstable communities consisting of group representatives, congressional committee and executive agency members, personnel, and advisers as well as 'policy watchers' (Heclo 1978). The role played by interest groups in the United States contrasts strongly with France where the political status of interest groups within the national policy-making networks is much weaker. As Hayward writes in his discussion of industrial policy-making, the products of the *Grandes Écoles* are 'regarded as entitled to influence public policy decisions because they embody a disinterested and elevated conception of the public interest. When pushed to extremes, this statism can amount to a desire to dominate all private group manifestations of a potentially disorderly society, prone to the seductions of sinister sectional interests' (Hayward 1986: 50). Consequently, in Suleiman's survey of the French administrative élite, senior civil servants initially found even the suggestion that groups influenced decisions offensive. This does not mean groups are excluded from the policy process, but rather which groups are included is a matter of discretion for the executive (Suleiman 1975: 327). In Hayward's (1986) terms they are 'pressure*d*' groups rather than pressure groups.

The main significance of this distinction for the character of the civil service is in its impact on the role of bureaucrats in policy-making. In a system where the executive dominates and can exclude groups from the policy-making process, or include them on its terms, the role of the civil servant is different from a system in which the bureaucrat is one player among many others. In the former, senior officials make decisions or advise those who make decisions; in the latter, they are more cautious participants in a wider game of bureaucratic politics in which outcomes are more likely to be negotiated among governmental and non-governmental actors.

4. ANALYSING THE EU BUREAUCRACY

These four components of character are related. The fragmentation of the American executive is closely related to its permeability since Congressional power in the US system of government both reinforces fragmentation and allows greater opportunities for interest groups to shape executive decision-making than the 'reactive' legislatures of Europe (see Mezey 1979). The cohesion of a bureaucracy is affected by the degree to which its members form a caste. These four components of the character of civil-service systems have not been set out as the basis of a classificatory system of bureaucracies. Rather, as the key parts of descriptions of civil-service systems in Western nations, they focus attention on major questions which need to be addressed when asking about the character of the EU civil service. Cohesion, the institutionalization of political control, the nature of the EU civil service as a caste, and its permeability not only allow us to define with more precision what we are looking for in the wealth of possible detail that could be unearthed about administrative life in Brussels, it also suggests some testable hypotheses about how these features might be related to the role of bureaucracy in the policy-making process of the EU.

Exploring such dimensions cannot 'predict' the circumstances under which bureaucrats will take a particular political stance on a particular political issue. Neither can such an exploration be used as a basis for an assessment of the power of officials, whether overall or with a specific decision or set of decisions. These dimensions can point to regular features of the interactions between civil servants and the wider political communities they serve, as well as of the interactions among civil servants.

Chapters 2 and 3 focus upon the fragmentation of bureaucracy in Brussels. In many respects the EU bureaucracy may be expected to be like any other complex government organization having diverse organizational units. Yet there are two features of the EU bureaucracy which might be expected to increase the fragmentation of the EU bureaucracy. The first is that the EU is a multinational institution. One of the characteristic problems of multinational bureaucracies is that of 'welding together men and women of different nationalities, languages and cultural traditions into an efficient administrative team' (Claude 1956: 179). Compared with other multinational institutions such as the United Nations, this diversity might not be such a problem. As Claude (1956: 179) writes of the League of Nations Secretariat, it

> remained from first to last predominantly a collection of Europeans and therefore a relatively homogeneous institution in important respects. Switzerland, as host country, provided the bulk of lower-level employees; Britain and France supplied the core of the professional staff, its standard languages, and its administrative techniques. The differences between these two linguistic and technical

contributions were real, but in the retrospection of the United Nations era they appear minor.

Nevertheless, as a former Director General responsible for personnel in the EU commented (Hay 1989: 27):

> Language is the expression of a culture; national thought processes are not identical. So meetings take longer, and more effort is required to understand, and to cope with situations in which misunderstandings come to light. . . . In addition, cultural differences affect management styles. Many officials feel some inhibition about exercising management in as direct a way as they would do in a single culture, because they are not certain that their colleagues of different nationalities share an identical approach to questions of authority, discipline and so forth.

A second feature of the EU system that leads to fragmentation is the absence of a focus of authority. Unlike most West European democracies (but in a similar manner to the United States) political authority itself is fragmented throughout EU institutions. In the United States the separation of powers between Congress and the Presidency means that individual sectors of the bureaucracy must build political support outside, making them parts of functional policy communities or 'subgovernments' rather than a collective single executive organization. Leaving aside the judiciary, political authority in the EU is in a similar way dispersed among the Council, the Commission, and, to an increasing extent, the European Parliament. 'This creates a high degree of autonomy of policy networks in EU governance . . . The Commission must usually consult an eclectic array of actors: private and public, national and supranational, political and administrative. Most EU policies reflect compromise between multiple institutions, member states and interest groups' (Peterson 1995: 78). This fragmentation is further reinforced by the absence of direct executive powers for most EU services. Policy is implemented by national civil services, opening up even wider possibilities for interests within member states to play a role in the policy process.

Chapter 4 looks at whether the top officials in the EU form a distinctive caste. It focuses upon the question of whether there is emerging within Europe a new, distinctive group of officials, as distinctive in their way as are the trained lawyers of Germany, the *Énarques* of France, or the Oxbridge arts graduates at the top of the British civil service. In doing so it examines the social characteristics of EU officials as well as their career patterns.

Chapters 2, 3, and 4 draw heavily upon data on European officials compiled from biographical sources, notably entries in *The European Companion* (London: DPR Publishing 1992 and 1993 edns.) and *Euro Who's Who* (Brussels: Editions Delta 1991), referring to officials in post in 1992 or 1993. Data was collected for 2,300 officials in all EU institutions, predominantly in positions corresponding to grades A4 and above. The extent to which career and background details were available varied from official to official. For some officials little more than name and position were available, and thus the number of valid observations we report in these chapters varies substantially. The data thus collected cannot be assumed to be a random sample of the higher levels of the EU service, and conclusions drawn from them must be treated with some caution. They do, however, provide important evidence which, where possible, is supplemented by other sources.

Chapter 5 looks at the role of interest groups within the European Union. In many respects the EU appears very similar to the US federal system in which executive officials have to secure support from political leadership within the executive and legislative branch, and this fragmentation of authority makes them especially susceptible to interest-group influence. In other respects, above all the numerical preponderance of business groups, the conditions prevailing within Brussels might suggest the possibility of a more traditional European group–state relationship: corporatism. Such a model implies a much stronger role for the European civil service in the policy process. Chapter 5 explores such models of group–EU relationships in the light of available evidence and from the perspective of the implications that each model has for the role of the bureaucracy in the decision-making process.

Chapter 6 looks at the institutionalization of political control within the EU. This issue is highly complex, because our conceptions of political control in European nation states are dominated by our conception of the minister. As Rose (1987: 22) writes, ministers 'are the chief group meant to give legitimate direction to government in a representative political system'. In the EU there is no exact equivalent of a minister—a politician who occupies senior executive office generally as part of a career in electoral party politics as a result of his or her party remaining in office. Commissioners, perhaps the closest equivalent, are nominees of the government of their home state. The differences between ministers and commissioners can sometimes be exaggerated: some ministers in member states have been appointed to office without having pursued a career in politics; or have sought elective office more or less as a formality. Moreover, as will be shown in Chapter 5, most commissioners themselves have pursued a successful career in party politics.

Although the College of Commissioners as a whole has to be approved by the European Parliament, the central difference between the commissioner and the minister is that the commissioner does not owe his or her position to a party majority in the legislature and the responsibility of a commissioner to the legislative body is far more limited than that of a minister. While this relationship with the European Parliament complicates the notion of 'political control', it is possible to see the commissioner as one focal point of political control within the EU.

The fragmentation of authority further complicates the notion of political control since the simple line of political control from parliament through minister to bureaucracy does not apply. Instead, political control can be exercised in principle by at least three major actors: member state governments and the European Parliament in addition to the minister. Chapter 6 focuses upon the commissioners and the way in which their political control is institutionalized through the *cabinet* and also explores whether there are other forms of 'politicization' through the institutionalization of some form of political control by member states, above all by the committees which come under the name of *comitologie*.

The concluding chapter reviews the evidence in the light of the four components of bureaucratic character framework. It goes on from this to re-examine traditional views which suggest that the European civil service acts as a 'brake' on political initiative within the European Union. The constitution of the European Union gives the Commission, and thus the civil service of the Commission, a significant policy-initiation role. In addition, a system of diffuse political supervision ensures that many of the apparently routine Commission decisions and regulations giving effect to Council legislation are subject to intergovernmental and interinstitutional bargaining and negotiation. The different roles of the Commission and the institutional environment in which it operates generate different types of bureaucratic activities for its members and civil servants. In each of these activities there are characteristic constraints on officials to act independently. In the conclusion these constraints are examined and their implications for a 'democratic deficit' are discussed.

2

The European Union—One Civil Service or Many?

1. THE EUROPEAN UNION AS A LARGE ORGANIZATION

Monnet recognized he had failed to create a small lean bureaucracy along the lines of the Commissariat du Plan as soon as the European institutions he had done so much to create had started life. In the first years of its operation the European Coal and Steel Community had over 550 full-time employees, and called on the services of over 1,500 part-timers and consultants through its network of advisory committees (Merry 1955). By 1955 there were more than six times as many in the High Commission of the European Coal and Steel Community (Merry 1955). At that time Léon Daum, a member of the first High Commission, bantered with Monnet over his statement that a High Authority with over 200 officials would be a failure: 'Now we're six times as many . . . and we're still succeeding' (Monnet 1978: 405). By 1958 there were 6,500 European civil servants (Daussin 1959: 144). In 1995 the official establishment of the institutions of the European Union stood at 28,035. Taking the direct employees of the major institutions of the EU alone (i.e. excluding the officials in the research institutes and agencies such as the Office for Official Publications which had an establishment of 4,098 officials or 15 per cent of total EU employment in 1995), Fig. 2.1 shows there has been an increase of 466 per cent over the past 25 years, from just under 4,000 in 1967 to nearly 24,000 in 1995.

Official European Community information sources tend to emphasize that the European Union administration is small; the usual comparison is it that it has around the same number of employees as a large municipality (Commission 1993: 1). Direct comparisons with such organizations miss the point that the EU has no substantial body of direct service providers, as found in a municipality with its teachers, social workers, and street cleaners. Whichever way one looks at it, the

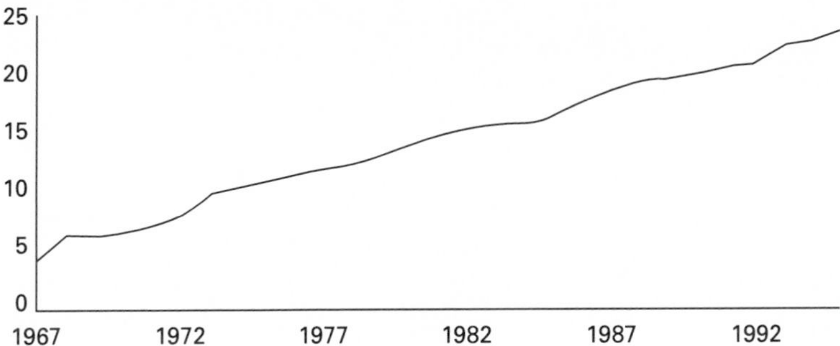

FIG. 2.1. *European Union staff (temporary and permanent), 1967–1995 (000s)*
Source: Annual budgets of the EEC/EC/EU.

EU has a sufficiently large civil service that it cannot be organized in the simple and cohesive form envisaged by Monnet: it is a large complex organization. In what sense, if not that originally envisaged by Monnet, is it a cohesive organization? In part this question can be addressed by looking at the degree to which the institutional structure of the EU forges a single civil service; in part it can be answered by looking at less formal divisions. Let us first look at the formal dimensions of the EU administration's cohesion and diversity.

2. A COMMON EU SERVICE

The most concrete form in which one can speak of a cohesive European civil service is in the determination of pay. The European civil service has a common grading structure for the staff of its major institutions.[1] Employees are divided into five main grade bands: A, B, C, D, and an LA band for translators and interpreters. The A grade is the most senior; it is also the band with the second largest number of officials (28.3 per cent of the European Union establishment is in band A), coming behind band C (34.7 per cent)—a category dominated by clerks and typists (Table 2.1). Each band is subdivided into different points. In the A grade there are eight points—A1 to A8. While they do not invariably correspond to rank within the EU, Director Generals and Deputy Directors General, the two most senior permanent posts in the Commission,

[1] With the exception of the European Investment Bank and the European Monetary Institute.

TABLE 2.1. *Percentage of employees (full and part time) in grade categories*

Grade	%
A	28.3
A1	0.2
A2	1.0
A3	3.1
A4	7.8
A5	7.1
A6	4.7
A7	4.2
A8	0.2
LA	11.7
B	19.7
C	34.7
D	5.4
TOTAL*	99.8

* Adds up to less than 100 due to rounding.

Source: *Official Journal of the European Communities*, L369, 37 (31 Dec. 1994), 154–77.

as well as the equivalent rank in the other institutions, are grade A1; a Director or Principal Adviser is A2, a Head of Unit is usually grade A3 but grades A4 and A5 can fill this position. Grades A1 and A2 are generally dominated by those who have been 'parachuted' into the higher levels from outside the European civil service, and A3 officials are a mix of parachutists and those who have come up through the ranks (see Ch. 3). The title 'Principal Administrator' (alternatively this position may have the title of head of section or deputy head of unit) is usually associated with grade A4 and to a less extent A5. As will be discussed in the next chapter, A4 is generally the most senior grade largely filled by permanent civil servants who have made their careers in the European service: i.e. those who have not been parachuted.

For the purposes of the common pay system within each grade, officials are placed on a step. For each grade there are generally eight steps (for a discussion of pay see Page and Wouters 1994*b*). Each official in all the institutions is for pay purposes placed at one point on a common matrix of 122 grades and steps. The pay matrix, which is upgraded at least annually, applies to all employees across all EU institutions: Council, Commission, courts, Parliament's secretariat, as well as the European University Institute and scientific research institutes. Moreover, the matrix is presented along with weightings taking account of cost of living variations throughout the world, so that EU officials everywhere are paid on the basis of a single pay deal. The matrix also directly determines the pay of commissioners, judges, and other top officials, since their salaries are calculated as multiples of the top step of the top grade (A1 step 6).

The process of salary setting is a common EU process. The current system of amending pay involves the compiling of statistics (supplied by statistical offices of member states, and passed on to the Commission), reflecting the costs of living for officials in Brussels, changes in the purchasing power of salaries in the national civil services, and the purchasing power of salaries in Brussels relative to other locations where EU officials are employed. The Commission makes a proposal to the Council of Ministers based on these data, using an agreed formula. The Commission's proposals pass through the Concertation Committee ('CoCo'), chaired by the Secretary General of the Council with representatives from the member states and from the staff; the Commission and other EU institutions may send observers. There are EU-wide allowances for employees, such as the expatriate allowance or the dependants' allowance.

Staff are involved in discussing and adjusting technical aspects of the operation of the formula as well as the draft of the Commission's proposals which go to the CoCo through the *Groupe Technique de Rémunération*, a group that ranges freely across a number of technical issues that emerge from the application of the formula—looking for example, at the effect on the joint indicator of moving Germany's capital from Bonn to Berlin (since it is calculated on the basis of officials' costs in national capitals) or the anomalies that creep in when the assumptions on which each member state's statistical office bases its contribution to the joint index differ.

There are also special taxes for EU employees: a Community Tax and a 'temporary contribution'. The Community Tax is a progressive tax: for each band of income a differential percentage is paid (Peeters 1968). Tax-deductible expenses and allowances are common to all EU employees. Since a budget crisis in 1981 there has been a second EU tax. The 'crisis levy' was introduced from July 1981 for a period of ten years. After 1991, and substantial industrial action by EU civil servants, the crisis levy was replaced by a 'temporary contribution', again to expire after ten years, set at a rate of 5.83 per cent.

For recruitment there are service-wide procedures. Recruitment is conducted by similar procedures across the institutions of the EU, though nevertheless separately. For the senior A category, entry into the EU administration usually takes place on the A8 or A7 level[2] and this by participation in the *concours*—a competitive examination. In the Commission the annual A8 *concours* is generalist and intended for young graduates without prior professional experience. It consists of preselection tests, one covering mainly general knowledge of Europe and European culture and another testing basic language skills. Successful candidates are then invited for interview in Brussels in front of a panel. The interview panel establishes a list of 'most suitable candidates'.[3] People on the reserve list are not automatically recruited into the EU administration. The reserve list remains valid for one year, but this period is frequently extended. When a vacancy occurs, the list is searched for candidates with a suitable background in terms of education or experience. It is also common for candidates themselves to start lobbying the services in which they would like to serve.

There are *concours* at higher levels in the Commission. The A7/A6 *concours*, organized every other year, aims to recruit people with at least two years of relevant professional experience, and the exam concentrates on specific professional areas (economics/statistics, law or public administration, and management). It is possible to enter directly into the A5 or A4 grades, although entry at this level is generally the result of temporary officials converting to permanent positions (temporary posts accounted in 1995 for 10 per cent of A grade Commission administrative employees, 37 per cent of Parliament A graders, 22 per cent A grade staff in the Court of Auditors, and 54 per cent of officials of the European Courts).

In addition there is a common set of promotion procedures within the major EU institutions. In the Commission every employee in the lower and middle levels of A grades automatically climbs a step in his or her grade each year. When an official reaches the top of the grade he, or she, remains there until promotion to the next grade. The formal decision on promotion to the next grade is taken by a *paritaire* committee,

[2] Council only recruits at A7 level.

[3] For the A8 and A7/A6 concours organized in Dec. 1993 over 50,000 people have registered all over the Community. Respectively 150 and 300 will be put on the reserve list, of which eventually 100 and 200 will be recruited.

in which the administration and the unions are represented. The actual procedure is based on a credit system which takes into account age, length of service, and merit. After two years of service as A8 one is put on a list, ranking all those eligible for promotion. Every year there is a quota of points available for promotions, which DG IX—the Directorate General responsible for personnel—distributes among the DGs according to the number of staff they have. These points are credited to civil servants on the basis of age, length of service in the rank, and merit. The first two are objective criteria. The last is open to interpretation. Formally the Director General is responsible for awarding points, but in practice the Directors usually decide. For an A8 to become A7 generally takes, in total, approximately six years (for a discussion of recruitment and promotion see Spence 1994).

3. THE EU AS A NETWORK OF ORGANIZATIONS

The European Union is a big organization, or rather a series of big organizations. Despite a common pay structure and similar recruitment and promotion procedures, the major institutions of the European Union—the Commission, the Council, the Parliament, the Economic and Social Committee, the Committee of the Regions, the Court of Auditors, the European Courts (the Court of Justice and the Court of First Instance)—each have their own separate administrative staffs. The European Investment Bank with 810 employees in 1993 is an independent organization within the EU. Although it was created by the 1957 Treaty of Rome, it is a bank owned by the fifteen member states with its own independent organization. While its precise position within the EU framework has been contentious (see Case 85/86, *European Court Reports* (1988), 1281–322) the EU staff grading structure and pay rates do not apply directly to it (see European Investment Bank 1994).

In addition to the longer established institutions, the EU heads of state or government meeting in December 1993 set up a series of 'new agencies'. The even distribution of these offices among countries outside France, Luxembourg, and Belgium as well as the circumstances of their birth led many to the conclusion that the whole exercise of creating and locating the offices was an example of 'pork barrel' politics at the European level (Abrahams *et al.* 1993). These institutions include the European Agency for Health and Safety at Work (Spain), the Office for the Harmonization of the Internal Market (Spain), the European

TABLE 2.2. *Employees of the European Union, 1995*

Institution	Employees
Commission	19,803
Administrative Staff	15,568
Joint Research Centre	2,080
Other Research Organizations	1,543
Office for Official Publications	465
European Foundation for the Improvement of Living and Working Conditions	71
European Centre for the Development of Vocational Training	76
Parliament	3,900
Council	2,378
European Court of Justice/Court of First Instance	837
Committees	659
Economic and Social Committee	128
Committee of Regions	74
Joint Services	457
Court of Auditors	458
TOTAL	28,035

Source: *Official Journal of the European Communities*, L369, 37 (31 Dec. 1994), 154–77.

Centre for Drugs and Drug Addiction (Portugal), the European Environment Agency (Denmark), the European Foundation for Training (Italy), the European Medicine Evaluation Agency (United Kingdom), the European Monetary Institute (Germany), the European Trademark Office (Spain), and the Europol Drugs Agency (Netherlands). The agreement also relocated CEDEFOP (the European Centre for the Development of Vocational Training) to Greece and split the the European Office for Veterinary and Plant Health Inspection from the Commission's administration and set it up as a separate agency in Ireland. The European Foundation for the Improvement of Living and Working Conditions remains in Dublin. The available information suggests that these agencies together will have around 1,000 employees (European Commission 1994*b*). In addition a new Translation Service is to be set up in Luxembourg. Most of the new agencies have self-governing boards, members of which are nominated by member states as well as by the institutions of the European Union. Some of them, such as the European

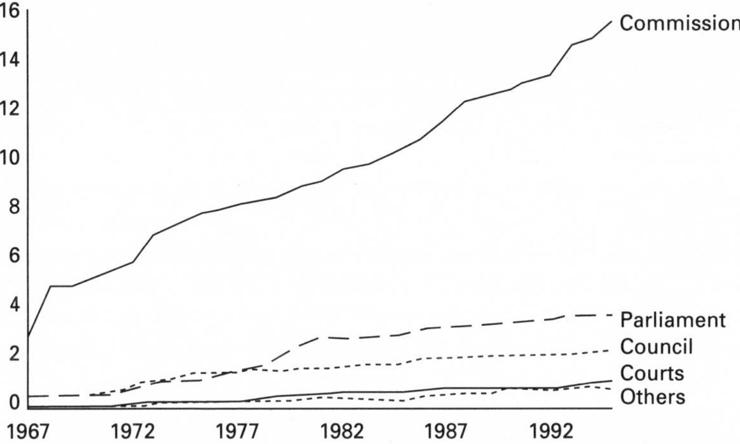

FIG. 2.2. *Employees (temporary and permanent) in EU institutions, 1967–1995 (000s)*

Source: Annual budgets of the EEC/EC/EU.

Medicine Evaluation Agency, will be financed only in part by the EU budget (European Commission 1994*c*; 1994*d*).

The Commission has always been the largest of the institutions in the number of employees (19,803 full- and part-time employees in 1995), followed by the Parliament (3,900), the Council (2,378), the Courts (837), and the Economic and Social Committee and Committee of Regions (659) which share central services. Despite some popular folklore to the contrary, there is no evidence of any single organization growing rapidly at the expense of others. Fig. 2.2 sets out the numbers of EU officials employed by each major institution since 1967. After direct elections to the European Parliament, in 1979 there was a substantial growth in EU officials employed by the Parliament, which overtook the Council in the size of its establishment. Growth rates for all the institutions tend to reflect changes in the constitutional environment of the EU, the biggest growth rates across all institutions occurring in 1968 (an increase of 47.9 per cent over 1967), as the newly merged European Economic Community institutions were being built up, and in the early 1970s when Britain, Ireland, and Denmark joined the EEC (in 1972 the growth over the preceding year was 13.9 per cent and in 1973 21.0 per cent). Historically the category including the Economic and Social Committee, the Committee of the Regions, and the Court of

Auditors has had the largest average growth rate over the period (9.2 per cent), followed by the Courts (8.2 per cent) the Parliament (7.9 per cent), and the Council (5.9 per cent). The Commission's average growth rate of 6.7 per cent is the second lowest of the major institutions.

While the powers of the EU institutions are based upon common treaties, above all the Treaty of Rome (1957), the Single European Act (1986), and the Maastricht Treaty (1992), each of the institutions has its own separate basis for authority. The ultimate basis of legitimacy of the Council rests with the national representatives of member state governments; for the Parliament authority derives from the direct election of its members, while the authority of the Courts, Court of Auditors, Commission, and the Economic and Social Committee and Committee of the Regions is derived from separate formal legal rights and obligations set out above all in the three major treaties.

The organizational structure of the EU institutions, like those of most nation states, arises from a mixture of, among other things, historical inheritance, past and present internal political conflicts, the construction of legislation, as well as fashions in organizational thinking. The largest of the EU institutions, the Commission, consists of twenty-three directorates general with defined responsibilities: similar to the number of separate ministries (as defined by government departments with ministers of Cabinet rank) found in member states.[4] The number of directorates general has grown by only three since 1972. Of the twenty-three directorates general, sixteen are identical or very similar in functional responsibilities to those created in 1972, although among this group of relatively stable directorates general there were some changes. For example, DG VI lost fisheries in 1977; DG X contained the Spokesman's Group for a while in the 1970s, but before and after this interlude it was a commission organization outside any DG, and DG III gained the functions of a disbanded DG XI (Internal Market) in 1977. The seven current DGs without direct counterparts in 1972 reflect expanded areas of EU activity either through developing new policy areas (environment and nuclear safety in DG XI; customs and indirect taxation in DG XXI; enterprise policy, distributive trades, tourism, and co-operatives in DG XXIII; telecommunication, information industries, and innovation in DG XIII), or through giving prominence to activities that had been

[4] This discussion does not incorporate the changes made after spring 1995 which include the creation of a DG IB, restructuring DGs I and IA, and the conversion of the old Task Force, Human Resources, Education, Training and Youth to new DG XXII Education, Training and Youth.

subsumed under those of other DGs (DG XIV for fisheries, and DG XV for financial institutions and company law).

Since the EU has fewer functional responsibilities than national governments of member states, directorates general are somewhat more specialized than most ministries. There are two separate directorates general (DG I and DG IA) for external relations (external *economic* and *political* relations respectively), the Directorates General of Agriculture (DG VI) and Fisheries (DG XIV) have functions carried out generally by single ministries in European nation states, and most of the functions carried out by DG III (Industry) and DG IV (Competition), DG XV (Financial Institutions and Company Law), DG XVIII (Credit and Investments), DG XIX (Budgets), DG XX (financial control), DG XXI (Customs and Indirect Taxation) would be carried out by only two or three ministries within nation states. The organization is less specialized where the responsibilities of the EU are fewer, such as the DG V (Employment, Industrial Relations, and Social Affairs), and some traditional ministries of member states such as interior, defence, health, social security, education have divisions within DGs rather than whole DGs as their closest counterparts within the EU.

Like most national government ministries, the real action in policy-making takes place not at the level of the DG as a whole, but much lower down within the organization, and like national bureaucracies, the organization of DGs is highly fragmented: relative to the number of its employees, it is divided into a large number of divisions (146) and units (708).[5] Whether staff identify more closely with the unit or the directorate or some other level of organization is difficult to determine on the basis of current research. The answer is likely to depend upon the directorate general concerned. Research has shown that within DG XV the division into two parts, financial institutions (division A) and company law, company, and capital movements taxation (division B) defines two bodies each with an *ésprit de corps*, yet many of the units within a directorate have different tasks, such as units concerned with tourism and charities within Directorate A of DG XXIII (Wilks 1992).

The administrations of the other institutions have similar divisions. The Council secretariat has a central services section divided into a private office, information, policy and documentation, and a legal service, and seven Directorates General (A to G) with five covering specific groups of functional concerns, one for personnel and administration

[5] The data and divisions here refer to 1993.

TABLE 2.3. *Organizational divisions of the Commission, 1993*

Organization	Employees	Divisions	Units	Staff per Division (1988)	Staff per Unit (1988)
DG IX Personnel and Administration	2,536	4	33	634	77
DG XII Science, Research, and Development (including Joint Research Centre)	2,486	18	82	138	30
Central Translation Service	1,678	8	71	210	24
DG VI Agriculture	826	10	41	83	20
DG VIII Development	766	6	37	128	21
DG I External Relations	613	12	37	51	17
Central Joint Interpreting and Conference Service	506	2	18	253	28
DG XIII Telecommunications, Information Industries, and Innovation	492	6	40	82	12
DG III Internal Market and Industrial Affairs	430	6	30	72	14
DG XVII Energy	409	7	20	58	20
DG X Audiovisual, Information, Communication, and Culture	369	3	24	123	15
Central Statistical Office	352	6	27	59	13
Central Secretariat General	335	8	24	42	14
DG IV Competition	309	5	26	62	12
DG V Employment, Industrial Relations, and Social Affairs	295	5	24	59	12
DG XIX Budgets	260	3	17	87	15
DG II Economic and Financial Affairs	231	6	22	39	11
DG XXI Customs and Indirect Taxation	229	3	17	76	13

DG XVI Regional Policy	196	5	16	39	12
Central Legal Service	170	0	0	na	na
DG XIV Fisheries	164	4	15	41	11
DG XX Financial Control	164	3	15	55	11
DG VII Transport	127	4	16	32	8
DG XI Environment, Nuclear Safety, and Civil Protection	119	3	17	40	7
DG XVIII Credit and Investments	101	2	9	51	11
DG XV Financial Institutions and Company Law	82	2	7	41	12
DG XXII Coordination of Structural Policies	60	1	5	60	12
DG XXIII Enterprise Policy, Distributive Trades, Tourism, and Cooperatives	56	2	7	28	8
Central Task Force, Human Resources, Education, Training, and Youth	55	1	5	55	11
Central Security Office	55	0	0	na	na
Central Spokesman's Service	52	0	0	na	na
Central Consumer Policy Service	40	1	4	40	10
Central Euratom Supply Agency	23	0	2	na	12
TOTAL	14,586	146	708	100	21

Note: This differs from the DG structure of 1995 in two main ways: DG XXII no longer exists, and DG IA is responsible for external *political* relations while DG I has responsibility for external *economic* relations.

Source: European Commission, *Directory of the Commission of the European Communities* (Brussels, Commission of the European Communities, 1993); Hay (1989).

(Directorate General A) and another for relations with other institutions (Directorate General F). The Parliament secretariat has central departments for data processing and legal services, and seven Directorates General. One of them covers the major functional committees of the European Parliament (DG II), while the other six cover general services to the European Parliament, such as information and public relations (DG III) and translation (DG VII). The Court of Justice and Court of First Instance are serviced by a central administration (with a registry and finance, personnel, information, and administration offices), a library, research, and documentation directorate, and a translation directorate. The Court of Auditors is divided into three audit groups, serviced by separate administrative divisions, as well as a central services secretariat covering personnel and administration and external relations. The Economic and Social Committee is divided into a chairman's office, secretariats to service the three Economic and Social Committee groups, five Directorates, three of which cover groups of functional concerns (Directorates A, B, and C), and a Directorate General for Coordination, Translation, Production, and Internal Affairs.

4. MOBILITY IN THE EUROPEAN UNION

While there are some Community-wide rules about recruitment and promotion, it is a widely held view there is little mobility within the EU civil service (Bourtembourg 1987). However, we have relatively little systematic data about the careers of officials in member-state bureaucracies and few criteria by which to determine the degree of mobility that is normal or desirable. Moreover, such direct comparisons would be somewhat misplaced, since the major functions of the European Union remain narrower than those of a nation state. Factors such as the technical competence required to do a senior administrative job might be more important for promotion in the European Union than a national bureaucracy and might lead one to expect less mobility. Even so, the evidence does not suggest a striking lack of mobility within the European Union.

There is relatively little mobility between major European institutions; few people as a proportion of total EU employees have moved from one institution, such as the Commission, to another, such as the Council. The scope for interinstitutional mobility is limited by the dominance of Commission which accounts for nearly three-quarters of

EU employees. It is difficult to measure exactly how much mobility there is since the biographical data we gathered on officials in post in 1992 or 1993 is sometimes rather sketchy on employment history (see Ch. 1). If we take the officials who have worked their way from junior to senior positions without having been through a *cabinet*, we find that of the 218 Commission officials for whom information is available 171 (78.4 per cent) have worked within the Commission throughout their EU careers, a further thirty-six (16.5 per cent) worked for organizations which became merged with the Commission (the High Authority of the European Coal and Steel Community and Euratom), and only eleven (5.1 per cent) worked in other EU institutions in their careers. For the Council and Parliament the figures are much smaller, but indicate a greater propensity for interchange. Seven (25.0 per cent) of the twenty-eight senior non-parachuted Council officials from whom information was available had been employed in other institutions—only one of them came from the Commission, two came from the Courts, and four from the European Parliament. Of the thirty-three Parliament officials fifteen (45.4 per cent) had worked in other institutions. Only eight of the fifteen had previously been in the Commission. The Commission is less likely to recruit from other institutions, and relatively fewer officials are likely to leave it to work in another EU institution.

When critics write about the lack of mobility they tend to mean mobility as movement between the Directorates General of the Commission. A study in the 1980s (cited in Bourtembourg 1987: 505–9) suggested that of seventy-four A grade officials who had passed their *concours* in the early 1970s, forty-four remained in the same Directorate General, while twenty had changed Directorate General once, and ten had changed twice. The study looked at officials who were between ten and twelve years into their careers in the EU and most had reached the level of A5 or A4. A mobility rate of 40 per cent over ten or so years is not small by the little we know of international comparisons. In the Netherlands and Germany whole careers tend to develop within the same ministry. Moreover, for the more senior levels of the service our data show a much higher level of mobility. Of all 207 senior Commission administrative (i.e. excluding those in research centres) officials on whom we have data (see Ch. 1) who have worked their way through the ranks without being 'parachuted' or joining a commissioner's *cabinet*, 126 or 61 per cent had worked in another Directorate General. These figures indicate a significant degree of mobility at the senior levels.

5. A FRAGMENTING ADMINISTRATION?

Despite a nearly EU-wide set of pay and conditions of service, as well as a significant degree of mobility among those working in EU institutions, the fragmentation of the EU has been one of the most consistent criticisms of its administration. In 1979 the Commission published the results of an independent review body headed by Mr Dirk Spierenberg which set out to 'examine how the Commission's organization and staff resources can best be adjusted to meet future needs, and thus cope with a rapidly changing workload' (Spierenberg 1979).

Spierenberg emphasized the importance of the national dimension as a major cause of fragmentation, above all in the College of Commissioners. The commissioners are designated by their national governments. They may thus have widely varying political backgrounds, they are most unlikely to know each other before taking office, and they are unlikely to conceive of themselves as members of a team. Moreover, there is, Spierenberg argued, an imbalance in the distribution of portfolios among commissioners, with some having a range of politically sensitive issues while others have a more limited set of more humdrum responsibilities. The president is a *primus inter pares*, and has only his personal authority to support his leadership. On the whole the Commission lacks overall cohesion and co-ordination.

The report was critical of the large number of basic administrative units (divisions and specialized services). It made detailed suggestions about how the problems of political and administrative fragmentation within the Commission could be addressed, including organizational consolidation. It proposed reducing the number of Directorates General from nineteen to twelve and then to ten, changes in the recruitment and career structure, making mobility within the EU civil service a prerequisite for a senior career path, strengthening the power of the Commission's presidency through a 'Screening Group' to assist him in giving overall direction to the Commission, encouraging forums for inter-DG contacts and improving the communication between the commissioner and his Directorates General. Most famous was the suggestion the number of commissioners' portfolios should be limited to eight with more or less equal weight. Even with further enlargement (the report was written just before the accession of Greece, and before the accession of Spain and Portugal) the number of commissioners should not rise above ten.

TABLE 2.4. *Organizational fragmentation in the European Commission, 1970–1995*

	1970	1975	1980	1985	1990	1995
Commissioners	9	13	13	14	17	20
Directorates General and similar*	20	19	19	22	24	25
Services outside DG structure**	7	10	9	9	10	10
Directors (A2)	98	110	116	126	146	166
Total Commission	5,273	7,803	8,885	10,429	12,887	15,568

* Includes organizations in the DG structure headed by a Director General (e.g. Enlargement Task Force).

** Secretariat, Spokesmen's Group, Joint Research Centre as far as they are not integrated in the DG structure.

Source: European Commission, *Directory of the Commission of the European Communities* (Brussels, Commission of the European Communities, various years).

At the heart of the Spierenberg criticism of the European Union administration, and of the problem of doing much about it, is the recognition that member states want to have officials who are their nationals in positions of power. Thus each member state expects to have at least one commissioner and to be able to place senior officials in the EU administration. A somewhat jaundiced view of the importance of national fair shares in the fragmentation of the Commission's organizational structure was provided by an official who argued: 'Jobs for the boys, that's what the member states want. If another top bod has to be found, they simply create another DG. By 2004 we'll have DG57 for cauliflower growers, probably with a Turkish Director General' (*Guardian*, 30 July 1993). It is a common enough criticism of the European Union to argue that it is prone to what may be termed a 'political' impulse to become increasingly fragmented.

The evidence on organizational structure does not support the argument that fragmentation is increasing particularly rapidly or that the arrival of new members causes it. Certainly new member states swell the number of commissioners, which increased when Britain, Ireland, and Denmark joined in 1973, in 1981 when Greece joined, in 1986 when Spain and Portugal became members, and again in 1995 with the accession of Finland, Sweden, and Austria (see Table 2.4). Yet this

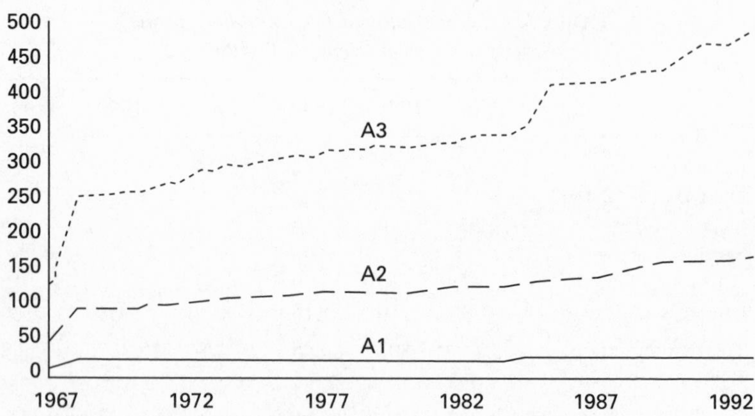

FIG. 2.3. *The growth of top jobs in the Commission, 1967–1995*
Source: Annual budgets of the EEC/EC/EU.

expansion of membership has a less perceptible impact on the number of organizational divisions. The number of Directorates General or similar organizations has grown only modestly, from twenty to twenty-five by 1995. Moreover, the pattern of growth does not suggest increased membership as a cause of increasing fragmentation. The 1973 expansion coincided with a *reduction* in the number of DGs from twenty to nineteen, although around the time of Spain and Portugal's accession in 1986 there was a net increase of two DGs, as three new DGs were created (Customs Union and Indirect Taxation, and Coordination of Structural Instruments) and the Task Force for Information Technology was brought back into the DG structure. Neither is a similar pattern of growth following increased membership to be found in the number of central service and other major organizational divisions outside the main DG structure. Measured by the total number of employees in the Commission, which grew around threefold over the period, the growth in the number of Directorates General appears modest.

Also modest by comparison to the total staff of the Commission is the increase in the number of A2 positions, a proxy for the number of directorates and similar organizational units, which has grown by 69 per cent over the twenty-five-year period (Table 2.4). Figure 2.3 shows that this nevertheless substantial increase has been the result of a longer term trend rather than a price to pay for enlargement. Figure 2.3 suggests that if there is an organizational price to pay for enlargement in addition to extra commissioners, the currency is more likely to be that of the unit rather than the directorate general or directorate since growth in the number of officials heading such organizational divisions seems to coincide more sharply with the advent of new members.

6. CONCLUSIONS

While one can point to formal internal divisions within the EU administration, it is important not to over-emphasize its distinctiveness in this respect. All administrative systems contain forces which generate fragmentation. Internal differentiation which produces such fragmentation is a basic feature of the division of labour which characterizes modern large organizations. Moreover, the emphasis upon policy networks and communities that one finds in much recent academic writing on the functioning of national administrations should lead one to discount the possibility of an organization such as the European Union being accurately described as a single monolithic whole, just as readily as one discounts such possibilities with the bureaucracies of its member states.

Some factors lead one to expect greater cohesion within the EU bureaucracy than one can find in those of member states. Not only is there a common pay system and conditions of work, there is some degree of mobility across sectors. Moreover, there is strong evidence that European Union officials share an enthusiasm for building the institutions of Europe and thus a sense of common purpose unlikely to be found in member state bureaucracies. In addition, the evidence of continual fragmentation through enlarged membership is not strong.

The Spierenberg linking of several of the problems of the European Union administration to nationality is nevertheless accurate. It was visible from the bargaining about the number and location of the 'new' institutions which came into being in 1995 (see p. 27 above) that member states viewed the location of an agency in their country, particularly those which appeared to have greater power, as a major prize. Ruud Lubbers's support for Amsterdam over Frankfurt as the location of the European Monetary Institute was reported to have cost him the Presidency of the Commission because of the German Chancellor, Helmut Kohl's irritation. Moreover, the staffing of the new agencies brought to light the clear support and pressure that member states bring to bear. A rare flavour of the type of bargaining engaged in by member states trying to insert their person in a top position was provided by leaked documents about the appointment of a chief and deputy chief of the newly created Europol police agency. A Belgian Interior Ministry memo suggested

> to the minister that he continues to support the classification of the candidates established by the interview committee. This approach would give the Belgian candidate the best chance. . . . If the nomination of two candidates from the Benelux causes a problem, then Belgium could support the British candidate . . . Our support for the British candidate could then bring together the non-Schengen votes [Britain, Denmark and Ireland] to elect our representative (*Guardian*, 10 June 1994).

The multinational character of the European Union is the source of some of the major distinctive features which mark off different groups of European civil servants from each other, and to which we must now devote our attention.

3

The Nationality Problem in the EU Administration

1. EXPERTISE VERSUS FAIR SHARES

While it is possible, as discussed in Chapter 1, to find many similarities between the administration of the EU and that of member states, or even of other nation states, the obvious distinctive characteristic of the administrative system of the EU is that it is a multinational bureaucracy. When considering the level of cohesion and differentiation within it, the impact of this basic fact cannot be ignored. Recruiting officials from different nationalities has an obvious and recognized direct impact, through creating distinctive linguistic barriers to communication within EU organizations. The multinational character of the EU also has less direct but no less important effects upon the internal structure of the administration and the career paths of its officials.

The European Union, like all international organizations, faces a dilemma. On the one hand, merit is a basic principle of modern organization—officials, especially those in senior positions, are appointed and promoted by virtue of their experience, qualifications, training, or demonstrated ability. On the other hand, civil servants come from nation states which traditionally like to see their countries are 'represented' in senior positions. We can speculate about the reasons for this—national pride would be visibly hurt if a country had very few or no top officials, a national government might feel it would be easier to influence or even just do business with top officials who speak the same language as its representatives and share the same culture. Or governments might believe officials trained in its country are simply better than any others. The issue of nationality is of fundamental importance to the character of the European civil service; and the way in which the EU deals with it has potentially far-reaching effects.

The principles of nationality and merit produce different approaches to appointment and promotion. One approach is to appoint or promote to the top positions the 'best' people on the basis of experience or some measure of competence or aptitude. This runs the risk of making some nationalities underrepresented and others overrepresented. Even if experience, competence, and aptitude are evenly spread across the nationalities who apply for EU jobs, some nationalities (above all Belgians and Luxembourgeois) are likely to have relatively larger numbers of applicants than others. Another approach is to set some sort of norm or quota for each nationality. In this case the risks are that those who are relatively less efficient or competent are appointed to top posts, and that career officials may feel thwarted when promotion to the top positions is denied them on the grounds of nationality. Both approaches find some support in the Staff Regulations governing EU employees. Article 27 sets out the desirability of 'geographical balance', as it requires that 'Recruitment shall be directed to securing for the institution the services of the officials of the highest standard of ability, efficiency and integrity, recruited on the broadest possible geographical basis from among nationals of Member states of the communities'. Article 29, on the other hand, expressly forbids nationality as a criterion for appointment or promotion.

In reality the strategy for recruitment does not come down on one side of this conflict between nationality and merit at the expense of the other. This chapter sets out how the European Union copes with the demands of these two contradictory approaches to handling nationals in a multinational bureaucracy, above all by distinguishing between two different levels in the service at which the nationality issue is addressed. Nevertheless, solutions to the difficulty of nationality generate problems of their own.

2. GEOGRAPHICAL BALANCE IN TOP POSITIONS

The pay and grading system of the European Union is designed to make EU employment attractive to nationals from all member states. The Commission is very sensitive to charges that it is an 'overpaid' bureaucracy, so the comparison of EU pay rates with those of national or other international civil servants is a sensitive issue. One of the dominant features of EU pay policy has been to secure geographical balance. This concern with geographical balance is reflected in the fact that EU pay is generally substantially above levels paid to home civil servants, although below diplomatic civil service pay rates (Personnel and Administration 1992: 39; *Courrier du personnel*, 8 (4 Mar. 1993), 2). A survey of salaries in the early 1990s found that top EU officials were paid around 37 per cent more than the highest paid national officials in member states (i.e. German officials) and over double their direct counterparts working for the Belgian state (Hood and Peters 1994: 27). The high priority given to attracting and retaining top officials from all member states can also be seen in the elaborate formula used to upgrade salaries annually, which takes account of changes in the pay rates of all member states and maintains the purchasing power of officials wherever they are located in EU employment (Page and Wouters 1994*b*).

There are limits to the degree to which pay levels can be used to recruit top officials in sufficient numbers from each member state. Levels of remuneration provide a common set of incentives to take up a post in the EU service; moreover, it is unlawful to discriminate between officials from different member states in pay over and above the allowances officials receive for living outside their home states. Yet the disincentives which they must counterbalance vary nationally. The most obvious cause of variation is national differences in pay for civil servants and other professionals: for professionals from some states an A4 or A5 salary is attractive, for others it is not. The Commission's own research found evidence of a clear relationship between pay rates in the home state and applications to the EU and concluded there is a 'shortage of candidates from well-off member states; the institutions risk being unable to attract enough candidates, and good enough candidates, to ensure an adequate representation from these countries' (Personnel and Administration 1992: 23).

Aside from pay levels, the costs of moving to Brussels or another EU location vary from one country to another. In addition there are less direct causes of variation, such as the costs incurred by officials of different nationalities maintaining a 'national' diet, interrupting offsprings' schooling, phoning home, seeing friends, or buying newspapers. In a country such as Britain, where home-ownership is far more common than, say, Belgium or Germany, absence from the housing market is a further potential cost. The inability to speak French or Dutch is a further disincentive variably distributed. To set general pay levels to compete with domestic pay rates in the countries for whose officials the costs are highest would be expensive indeed.

For most positions within the EU there is a strong geographical imbalance in employment. We may show this imbalance using a 'fair shares' index based upon the difference between numbers of officials from each member state compared with the number of officials one would expect if employment were strictly proportionate to member state population. The index shows the size of the contingent of employees from each member state at each grade relative to the number of officials that would be expected if there were strict proportionality. Overrepresentation is indicated by positive values, underrepresentation by negative values, and a value of zero means levels of employment are exactly proportionate to population. On this basis, taking all Commission employees, Britain (–56), Germany (–56), France (–30), and Spain (–34) are substantially underrepresented in the Commission, Italy (–14) is moderately underrepresented, while Greece (+41), Denmark (+70), Ireland (+156), Belgium (+904), and Luxembourg (+1,754) are substantially overrepresented. It is hardly surprising that when one pays above German civil service wages to attract German applicants, many more Belgians and Luxembourgeois, with generally lower pay in their national government jobs and lower costs of moving, are attracted to the EU.

The overall index of disproportionality (ID) presented in Table 3.1 shows the degree to which there is over- or underrepresentation in different grades in the EU since it gives the average *magnitude* of the disproportionality at each grade and level (i.e. ignoring the positive or negative signs of the preceding columns) weighted by the number of officials from each nationality at each level to avoid the index simply overstating the impact of relatively smaller countries such as Belgium and Luxembourg. Generally speaking, the lower one goes in the EU hierarchy, the greater the disproportionality; the index of disproportionality increases from 82 in category A to 456 in category B, 680 in C, and 785 in D.[1] A similar pattern applies in the Council where the correlation between the index for grade A officials in the Commission and Council is +0.76, indicating that the countries under- or overrepresented in the Commission tend to be similarly under- or overrepresented

[1] Using no weighting or a population weighting factor produces very different results. No weighting makes the index extremely sensitive to the smaller countries, many of which have highly disproportionate numbers of officials. Weighting by population gives an index which reflects largely the underrepresentation of the more populous nations. Weighting by number of officials gives an indication of the level of disproportionality sensitive to the actual number of officials involved.

TABLE 3.1. *National proportionality in the Commission, 1993*

	D	UK	I	E	F	NL	P	GR	DK	IRL	B	L	ID
A	−37	−30	−24	−13	−1	+28	+32	+91	+91	+220	+321	+995	82
A1	−42	−21	−21	−2	+4	+120	−38	−36	+152	+253	+225	+1,656	92
A2	−33	−5	−13	−14	−11	+54	+73	+36	+165	+210	+59	+1,749	71
A3	−19	−9	−8	−31	+3	+12	+2	+23	+108	+169	+139	+1,685	61
A4	−23	−27	0	−49	+24	+9	−57	+4	+118	+247	+238	+1,321	73
A5	−48	−25	−37	+8	−12	+34	+34	+197	+91	+156	+363	+595	96
A6	−59	−35	−47	+5	−8	+18	+117	+133	−7	+179	+593	+552	162
A7	−36	−49	−33	+0	−9	+39	+81	+123	+85	+316	+349	+805	99
A8	−39	−44	−16	+38	−26	+96	+83	−4	+212	+250	+189	+770	46
B	−60	−61	−34	−22	−29	+41	−15	−1	+32	+145	+1,053	+2,631	456
C	−62	−68	−17	−53	−53	−50	+20	+21	+98	+150	+1,273	+3,614	680
D	−95	−95	+106	−64	−51	−77	−16	+46	−59	−77	+1,171	+5,266	785
TOTAL	−56	−56	−14	−34	−30	−6	+14	+41	+70	+156	+994	+1,574	269

Source: European Commission internal memorandum, 8 February 1993.

in the Council. In the Council, however, the level of over- and under-representation appears slightly higher than for equivalent grades in the Commission.

Geographical balance is a factor that applies generally in the A category. It is commonly regarded as a feature of grades A1–A3. In the directorates general it is normal for three or four Directors General (A1) to come from the larger member states while one or two come from the smaller countries. Positions at around the level of head of unit (A3) and above are generally associated with national fair shares since these sensitive appointments are the subject of consultations with the governments of member states, frequently resulting in 'parachuting' in officials from the outside or the rapid promotion of insiders. Geographical balance has been widely accepted in the higher reaches of the administration (but the more direct ways of achieving it have been declared illegal, see below). Yet Table 3.1 suggests it is not limited simply to this level. The index of disproportionality is significantly less in the A1–A3 category (ranging from 61 to 92 with an average of 75) than in the A4–A8 category (from 46 to 162 with an average of 95) indicating a less even balance at these lower levels. Nevertheless, at these lower levels there is still a far more even balance than in grades B, C, and D, and this suggests that geographical balance is sought lower down in the A category than A3.

An indication of whether imbalances in the A grades are the result of different numbers of applicants from each member state can be given by looking at the nationality of those who apply for EU A grade competitions (see Table 3.2). As one might expect the number of Belgian and Luxembourgeois applicants is over 500 per cent above the number one would expect on the basis of population (an overrepresentation of +514 and +4,466 respectively). In Germany there is four-tenths the number that population size alone would suggest (–60) and in Britain just over one-quarter (–73). The overall index of disproportionality for applicants is 130. This increases to 147 when one looks at laureats—those who pass the competition. While Germans and Britons have a higher success rate than many other countries, so do the Danes and the Belgians. Yet the number of A grade officials from each country is far more evenly spread, with an index of disproportionality of 82. This generally greater disproportionality among laureats than among A grade officials (with the exception of those at grade A6) suggests that geographical balance plays a role in selecting which laureats will actually be appointed to a post within the Commission.

TABLE 3.2. *National proportionality in the Council, 1994*

	D	UK	F	I	E	NL	P	GR	DK	IRL	B	L	ID
A	−35	−31	−24	−17	−16	+51	+81	+121	178	+247	+250	+762	80
B	−49	−62	−22	+30	−59	+36	+39	+9	42	0	+778	+395	228
C	−63	−69	−44	+9	−41	−1	+138	+158	352	+193	+674	+304	222
D	−97	−82	−82	+144	−49	−32	+67	−50	−100	−100	+1,131	+1,258	495
TOTAL	−60	−64	−42	+19	−41	+7	+114	+120	259	+154	+669	+450	206

N = 1693

Source: Internal Council memorandum (undated), figures refer to 1 January 1994.

TABLE 3.3. *Applications for A grade competitions and laureats, 1986–1991*

	B	L	IRL	GR	P	I	NL	DK	E	F	D	UK	ID
Applications	+514	+466	+145	+119	+63	+45	+12	−12	−15	−17	−60	−73	130
Laureats	+608	+345	+186	+96	−9	−4	+27	+98	−13	−30	−35	−62	147
A grade officials	+321	+995	+220	+91	+32	−24	+28	+91	−13	−1	−37	−30	82

Source: European Commission, *Recruitment Requirements in the Community Institutions* (Brussels: Nov. 1992).

TABLE 3.4. *Parachutists and career officials in the European Union*

	% career	% parachuted	N
Commission	49.1	50.9	725
Council	49.1	50.9	57
Parliament	51.8	48.2	85
Court of Auditors	30.8	69.2	26
Courts	31.9	68.1	47
ESC	64.5	35.5	31
TOTAL	48.5	51.5	971

Sources: Statistics compiled from entries in *The European Companion* (London, DPR Publishing, 1992, 1993 edns.); *Euro Who's Who* (Brussels, Éditions Delta, 1991).

3. PARACHUTING

While pay rates, recruitment procedures, and promotion policies may be sufficient to ensure an acceptable level of national representation in the European Union administration, there are far more immediate and direct ways of ensuring the nationals of a member state reach senior positions. Spence (1994: 74–86) outlines the major devices which include converting temporary posts into permanent ones and rigged *concours* (entry examinations). The most famous practice is known as parachuting—inserting officials or other candidates from outside the EU administration directly into senior positions within it. If we take as a working definition of a parachutist those people whose first job within the EU was in a senior position (a principal administrator in the Commission or above, and including a member of the *cabinet*), then of the senior officials of the 1993 and 1994 on whom data is available, just over one-half were parachuted into the European Union service (Table 3.4). Two-thirds of the senior officials of the Economic and Social Committee were career officials, whereas over two-thirds of the officials of the Court of Auditors and the European Courts were recruited directly from outside. In the major administrative institutions, the Commission, the Council and the European Parliament, almost one-half of top officials were parachuted on this basis.

While there are other methods of getting officials from a particular nationality into top positions, above all through rapid promotion, such methods are far less significant than parachuting outsiders in. The differences between parachutists and non-parachutists will be examined in more detail in the next chapter, but of the 270 non-parachutists from the Commission's Directorates General or central services covered in the biographical sources of 1992 and 1993, only four had served in the Commission for less than ten years, indicating a small number of officials indeed who make it to the top posts through rapid promotion. While this figure does not take account of those who come in at A3 level or as a *cabinet* member and are then promoted rapidly, it nevertheless accurately emphasizes the strict demarcation between longer serving career officials and parachuting officials, at least in their chances of reaching the top, and emphasizes the importance of parachuting in as a means of promoting favoured candidates to top positions.

While it is frequently assumed that parachuting is a matter of securing national balance, other considerations are also important; officials may be brought in among other reasons because they are admired for their skills or because they are politically close to a commissioner. In the late 1980s, Dieter Engel, a Canadian national, was appointed over two internal candidates (one German and one Luxembourgeois) Director in DG XVIII with responsibilities for investments and loans (see European Court of First Instance case 20/89: 13/12/90 and 16/12/93). Moreover, the process of parachuting an official into a top position is certainly not a matter of routine. There are standard procedures: consultative committees for A2 and A3 posts and formalities which must be observed if litigation is to be avoided. Nevertheless, such appointments may involve a highly contentious struggle between different member states for an important new position or they may be a routine replacement of a retiring official who is expected to be replaced by a fellow countryman (see the following section). Depending upon the level of seniority and the contentiousness of the issue, the process in the Commission is one of negotiation between a variety of groups and individuals that may involve prominent participants: senior officials in DG IX (the DG responsible for personnel), the Permanent Representatives, members of the Council, the commissioner responsible for the DG in which the appointment is sought, the commissioner responsible for DG IX, commissioners from the home state of the applicants, the President of the Commission, and the Vice President of the Commission.

Table 3.5 shows that the bulk of top officials at the level of Director General (A1) and Director (A2) are parachuted officials. The data in Table 3.5 do not necessarily mean officials were parachuted into the job

TABLE 3.5. *Grades of career and parachuted officials in the Commission (DGs and central services)*

Grade	% career	% parachuted	N
A1	18.2	81.8	33
A2	34.3	65.7	105
A3	55.1	44.9	354
A4 and below	66.7	33.3	54

Sources: *The European Companion* (London, DPR Publishing, 1992, 1993 edns.); *Euro Who's Who* (Brussels, Éditions Delta, 1991).

that they currently hold. While Willis (1982) suggests that 70 per cent of the top two grades were internal promotions, our data indicate those promoted were already in senior positions, having been parachuted in beforehand—as we will see in the next chapter, parachutists stay in the EU civil service for a long time and are not like the traditional picture of the American 'in and outer'. Around 70 per cent of the top two grades in the Commission are filled by officials who have been parachuted in from outside. Even lower down, at A3 level, 45 per cent of officials started their Commission career as senior officials. While the numbers are far fewer, and inferences consequently more hazardous, even below the A3 level a significant proportion of officials, our data suggest a third, are parachutists according to the defnition used here.

4. THE NATIONAL FLAGS SYSTEM

One way of parachuting officials into top posts is to use the 'national flags' system, according to which certain posts within a Directorate General are said to 'belong' to certain nations. This was described by Coombes as 'reserved posts', although he also included the possibility that appointment was made on the basis of political orientation as well as of nationality (1970: 131–2). The practice of reserving posts for nationals of a member state is explicitly outlawed by article 27 of staff regulations. The illegality of the system was underlined by the Court of First Instance in a decision of March 1993. The case shows how the 'national flags' system used to work at least in some cases.

In 1990 DG XIV had advertised three Director posts (A2) with responsibility for fishing policy. The three outgoing Directors were French,

Italian, and Spanish. A number of internal candidates (including the two plaintiffs—a German and a Dutchman—as well as a UK national) were rejected, and the consultative committee considering the vacancies decided to solicit applications from other candidates. The committee itself put forward names including the names of the three people (a Frenchman, a Spaniard, and an Italian) who were eventually appointed. The qualifications of the candidates, especially the Italian, did not match well those set out in the original job specification. The Italian candidate had no experience of fisheries policy, but was an economist who had worked for the Commission since 1970 in DG II (Economic and Financial Affairs) and had been made a deputy *chef de cabinet* to the Vice-President of the Commission, Filippo Maria Pandolfi, in 1989. The Court decided the appointments had been made unlawfully and annulled them. The Court decision did not spell the end for the principle of geographical balance. The Court did not disagree with the objective of geographical balance, but rather the way in which balance was achieved, through the simple replacement of a departing official by another of the same nationality.

The March 1993 case should not be taken as evidence that the 'national flag' system dominated in the Commission—its direct importance has been exaggerated (Johnson 1993). There is some evidence to suggest that the 'national flags' system operates at the level of the Directors General more strongly than at other levels. Coombes (1970: 132) showed that this system seemed to operate rigidly in the early years of the EU since 'up to the end of 1966 only one post of Director General—that for Administration—had changed nationality, and that was when a Belgian replaced a Dutchman in 1965'. Over time, with more member states and more opportunities for replacements, this practice of successors having the same nationality as outgoing Directors General has diminished. Nevertheless, Grant (1994: 95) suggests 'the Director General of financial services is always a Briton; that of agriculture, a Frenchman; that of competition policy a German; that of regional policy a Spaniard and that of economic and monetary affairs an Italian'. If we look at this claim more closely we may qualify this as a more general characterization of the way Directors General are appointed. Table 3.6 examines the nationality of Directors General since 1975 in those DGs which were not subject to major reorganization over the period. Most of these DGs have had Directors General of more than one nationality since 1975, although five—DG II, DG IV, DG VI, DG XVIII, and DG XIX—have had officials of the same nationality through-

TABLE 3.6. *The nationality of Directors General, 1975–1995*

	1975	1980	1985	1990	1995
DG I External Relations	NL	UK	UK*	D	D†
DG II Ec. and Fin. Affairs	I	I*	I*	I	I
DG III Int. Market & Ind. Aff.	vacant	L	L	L	I
DG IV Competition	D	D	D*	D*	D
DG V Empl., Ind. Rel., and Soc. Aff.	UK	B	B	B	UK‡
DG VI Agriculture	F	F*	F*	F	F
DG VII Transport	UK	UK	UK*	E	UK
DG VIII Development	D	D*	D*	D	DK
DG IX Personnel and Admin.	F	F	F*	UK	B
DG X Audovis., Inf., Comm., and Culture	IRL	I	D	F	L
DG XII Science, R&D	D	D	I	I	I
DG XIII Telecom, Inf. Ind., and Innov.	UK	UK	UK	F	F
DG XIV Fisheries	na	IRL	IRL	E	E
DG XV Fin. Inst. & Company law	DK	DK*	DK	UK	UK*
DG XVI Regional Policy	I	NL	NL	E	E
DG XVII Energy	B	UK	UK*	GR	GR
DG XVIII Credit and Investm.	I	I	I*	I	I
DG XIX Budgets	na	F	F	F*	F
DG XX Financial Control	I	I	I	NL	UK

* A different incumbent of the same nationality as the incumbent of five years before.

† For DG I there are currently two Directors General, one German and one Spaniard; the Director General in DG IA is also a German.

‡ Acting.

§ DGs which remained broadly similar over the period. Entries refer to incumbents in February of cited year.

Sources: Commission of the European Community, *Directory of the Commission of the European Communities* (Brussels, various years).

out (Table 3.6). The asterisked entries in Table 3.6 indicate changes in incumbency where the nationality is the same as five years before. Thus the long period of Italian stewardship of DG XVIII is a result of one change of Director General where one Italian replaced another. Incumbency of the post of Director General changed in thirty-nine cases out of a possible seventy-three in Table 3.6. Of these thirty-nine, fifteen changes (or 38 per cent) involved changes between incumbents of the same nationality and twenty-four (or 62 per cent) involved incumbents of different nationality. We know that national balance is most likely to operate at the very top level of the EU administration. Consequently we must bear in mind that to maintain the balance some Director General position in the near future is likely to be filled by a national from the country to which a recently departed belonged. It is therefore difficult to distinguish between the exercise of the 'national flags' principle and the more widely accepted principle of geographical balance. Nevertheless, in three cases DG II, DG IV, and DG VI, where at least two incumbent changes have been between officials of the same nationality (Italians, Germans, and French respectively), there appears to be a long tradition of the post going to a particular nation. That this might not be an iron law of top appointments is suggested by the fact that in DG VIII, Development, a long period of German incumbency was ended with the appointment of a Dane to the post in 1994.

Below the level of Director General there is not much evidence to support the view that much more than a minority of even the top positions is filled on this basis. It is difficult to take a very long-term view of the operation of this system since organizational change within the Commission makes it difficult to see precisely how far positions have been handed on to successors from the same nation state. However, if we look at the five-year period between 1988 and 1993, when the level of continuity in organization of the Commission is sufficient to allow a comparison, we can get an indication of the degree to which the national flags system has operated. Over this period the positions of Director General, Deputy Director General, or Director, may have (*a*) been filled by the same individuals for the whole period (no change); (*b*) been filled by different individuals but from the same member state (change, same nationality); (*c*) been filled by different individuals but not from the same member state (change, different nationality); (*d*) been held by only one individual for part of the five-year period, remaining unfilled after they have left office (vacant); (*e*) been held by only one individual for part of the five-year period but subject to major reorganization. Taking the Directors General, Deputy Directors General, and Directors in the Commission's DGs and the Secretariat General we find that of the sixty-two changes over the five-year period, eighteen (or 29 per cent) were filled by persons of the same nationality (Table 3.7). The numbers themselves are small, so any patterns detected can be only suggestive. Nevertheless, the national flag system seems to be more prevalent among DGs and Deputy DGs (around one in three changes are between officials of the same nationality) than

TABLE 3.7. *The 'national flags' system: continuity and change in incumbency of key Commission posts, 1988–1993*

	Directors General/Deputy Directors General	Directors
No change	22	58
Change, same nationality	7	11
Change, different nationality	12	32
Vacant/reorganized	15	33
TOTAL	56	134

Sources: *The European Companion* (1992, 1993); *Dod's European Companion 1990*; *Who's Who in the European Community and Other Institutions* (3rd edn., Brussels, Éditions Delta, 1986).

among Directors (around one in four). The French appear to dominate among those who pass the post to a compatriot—six of the eighteen posts which changed hands but to incumbents of the same nationality were held by French officials, as against three held by Italians, three held by UK citizens, two held by Germans, and the Netherlands, Ireland, Portugal, and Luxembourg having one each. This does not mean that nationalities within Directorates General are not consciously balanced. It does mean that the balance is generally achieved by somewhat more subtle means than passing on the national flag.

5. COLONIZATION

In some countries there has been a tendency for different ministries to be occupied by different political parties—for example, in Austria for much of the twentieth century (Neisser 1982: 241) different parties colonized different *Ressorts*. At the European Union level there is little evidence to suggest different DGs or other organizations have been allotted to different nations. Comparison of the weight of different nationalities among top officials in individual organizational units is difficult, since there are generally insufficient numbers in each unit for statistical comparison. However, it is possible to give a broad indication of the degree of overrepresentation of different nationalities at each level. Table 3.8 shows the number of senior officials included in the biographical sources (see Chapter 1), predominantly A4 and above,

TABLE 3.8. *Top officials in EU organizations*

	B	DK	NL	F	D	GR	IRL	I	L	P	E	UK	TOTAL
DG I	5	1	3	8	9	1	1	9	1		4	13*	55
DG II	3	1	2	4	4	1		6		2	3	1	27
DG III	6		1	8	13*	2	1	9	3	1	4	6	54
DG IV	3	1	1	4	9*	2	1	3	1	2	1	3	31
DG V	4		4	5	3	4		4			2	3	29
DG VI	2	3	3	9	7	2	2	7		2	2	10*	49
DG VII		1	1	1	3	3		2			2	1	14
DG VIII	2	1	1	8	9*		2	4	1	3	2	5	38
DG IX	6	1	3	9	3	3	1	11*	2	1	1	5	46
DG X	3	1		3	2			6	2		1	4	22
DG X (field offices)	1	2	1	3	2	1	2	5	2	3	2	3	27
DG XI	2	1	2	2	6*			3				3	19
DG XII	7	1	4	10	12*			16*		1		5	56
DG XIII	3	2	3	11	5	4	1	8	1		6	11*	55
DG XIV	2	2		1	1	1	1	2			2	1	13
DG XV	1		1	2	2	1		1	1			1	10
DG XVI		1		5	3	2		5		1	2	3	22
DG XVII	3	1	4	3	3	3	1	4			1	4	27
DG XVIII	1		1	2			2	4			1		11
DG XIX	1		1	4	4	1		8*			1	3	23

DG XX	3	1	1	2	3	1	1	2		1	1	2	18
DG XXI	1	2		3	4			3			1	5	19
DG XXII	1			2		1	1				1	2	8
DG XXIII				3	2	2	1	2				2	12
Spokesman's Service	1	1	1	3		1	1	1		1		3	13
Translation service	4	8*	4	2	9	8*		7		5	6	6	59
Commission Legal Service	1	1	2	6	5	1		4	1	2	3	3	29
Commission Stat. Service	4	1		5	6	1		4		2	1	5	29
Consumer Policy Service	4*	1									1		6
Forward Studies Unit	1			2	1			1			1		6
Joint Interpreting Service	2	1	1	1	5			2	1		1		14
Secretariat General	6*	1	1	5	7		1	8				4	33
Working Conditions Found.	2		1	1	1		2					1	8
Joint Research Centre	10*	1	3	9	13*			14*			1	3	54
Council Secretariat	4	8*	5	6	10	7*	4	8		5	7	12	76
Auditors	2	1	5*	7	4	1	1	6	1	1	2	3	34
Courts	5	3	3	7	7	4	2	6	3	4	4	5	53
EIB	7	5	6	16	20*	4	1	10	3	2	7	20*	101
Parliament Secretariat	4	8	4	23*	12	8	3	16	2	5	6	18*	109
ESC	2	1	2	4	3	3	1	3	1	2	3	9*	34

* At least three more top officials than would be expected if all officials from different nationalities were evenly spread throughout the EU.

Source: *The European Companion* (1992, 1993); *Euro Who's Who* (1991).

from each member state in each organizational unit of the EU administration. While the numbers in each cell are too small for statistical significance tests, Table 3.8 asterisks cases with three more top officials than one would expect if each nationality among officials were equally represented, as a rough indicator of possible overrepresentation.[2]

Overall Table 3.8 shows no general evidence of officials from single member states being given the larger part of the top jobs in different organizations. In no instance when there are more than ten top officials are more than half of the officials from a single member state. Taking the larger countries, Germans and Italians together form exactly one half of the top officials in the scientific research organizations of DG XII (Science, Research, and Development) and the Joint Research Centre in which they are both substantially overrepresented This dominance of Germans and Italians in DG XII is likely to be a result of the fact that significant numbers of senior officials are employed in German and Italian research institutes (such as the Institute for Transuranium Elements in Karlsruhe and the complex of research units at Ispra). In addition, Germany is substantially overrepresented in Commission DG III (Industry), DG IV (Competition), DG VIII (Development), DG XI (Environment, Safety, and Nuclear Protection), and the European Investment Bank; Italy in DG IX (Personnel and Administration), DG XIX (Budgets); France in the Parliament Secretariat; the United Kingdom in DG I (External Relations), DG XIII (Telecommunications), the European Investment Bank, the Parliament Secretariat, and the Economic and Social Committee (see Table 3.8). Among the smaller countries Belgium is overrepresented in the Joint Research Centre and the Consumer Policy service of the Commission, Denmark and Greece in the Translation Service of the Commission as well as the Council secretariat, the Dutch among the Court of Auditors, the Irish among Commission delegations outside Brussels.

The data discussed here do not add up to evidence of different parts of the EU administration being allocated to different countries. In fact the national distribution of top posts throughout the EU administration supports the view expressed in an interview by an official from DG IX

[2] Calculated on the basis of the number of officials in the data set; $O_i = N_i-((TN_a/TA)*T_i)$, where O_i is the level of overrepresentation in any particular organizational unit, N_i is the number of officials of a particular nationality in each organizational unit, TN_a is the number of officials of a particular nationality in all EU organizations, TA is the number of officials (of any nationality) in all EU organizations, and T_i is the number of officials of all nationalities in a particular organizational unit.

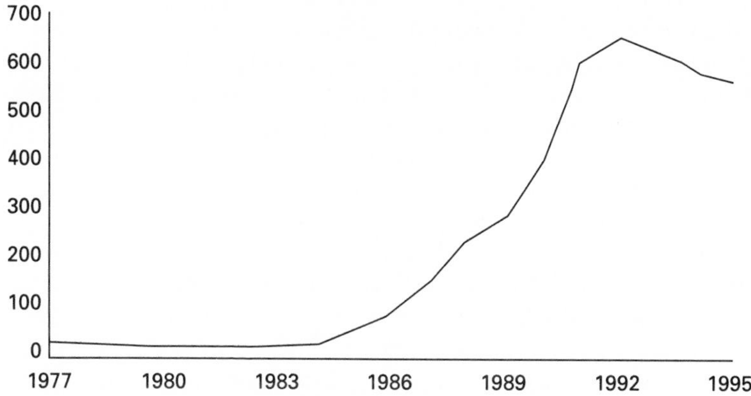

FIG. 3.1. *Secondments to the European Commission, 1977–1995*

Source: European Commission, *General Report on the Activities of the European Economic Community/European Community/European Union* (Luxembourg, Office for Official Publications of the European Communities, annual).

that DG IX attempted as far as possible to make sure that no two links in the hierarchical chain of command within the senior levels of the Commission were occupied by people from the same member state.

6. SECONDMENT, EXPERTS, AND EXTERNAL RESOURCES

One way around the limitations imposed by the need to maintain a geographical balance is to employ the people one wants within the Commission under terms that exclude them from official calculations of national balance. Perhaps the most commonly known way of doing this is through *détachement.* Since 1977 the Commission has hosted officials on secondment from employment in member states: they are known as *experts nationaux détachés*. They come mainly (but not exclusively) from public-sector organizations, primarily the civil services of member states. According to official figures, the number of seconded officials remained low (at around twenty) for the first ten years of the operation of the scheme. After the mid-1980s there was a rapid expansion, peaking at 650 in 1992, and tailing off shortly after, following demands by the European Parliament that the number of seconded civil servants be 'stabilized' (Fig. 3.1). The increased use of seconded officials has to some extent coincided with stringency within the institutional budget of the European Union. While the overall number of permanent establishment posts in the Commission has expanded, it has done so at a rate well below that requested by the Commission. Moreover, and this applies especially to the period 1986 to 1988 when the number of seconded officials grew from 89 to 240, many of the newly authorized establishment posts were 'reserved' for nationals of Portugal and Spain following enlargement.

Experts nationaux détachés are employed for a number of reasons. The most obvious is they are required to fill gaps in expertise within the Commission created by, among other things, new states joining the EU, the expansion of EU activities, and the difficulties of recruiting permanent staff with technical knowledge and experience in some specific areas, such as taxation, energy, or customs administration. They can be employed without raising questions of national fair shares in Commission posts. It is possible to reorganize parts of a Directorate General so the work formerly done by, say, an A3 official whose appointment might to require approval by a member state, can be done by seconded officials working alongside permanent officials below A3 grade.

Seconded officials are recruited generally from among those who have, as national civil servants, already had some contact with the Commission as part of their national civil-service duties. Frequently the seconded officials themselves approach counterparts within the Commission, indicating a wish to spend three years in Brussels. If appointed, the expert continues to receive a salary from the employer in the home state, and a supplementary allowance from the European Union. They tend to be employed in A grade jobs, often doing the sort of job one might find being done at around the A4 to A6 levels by an EU establishment official. If nearly all 565 seconded officials in 1995 are at grade A4 to grade A8 level, they make up around 12 per cent of the workforce at this level.

The European Parliament has been critical of the use of seconded national experts. Like European civil-service staff unions it sees them as a potentially dangerous move towards the 'nationalization' of the European administration—allowing its operation to become unduly influenced by member states. A report by the Committee on Institutional Affairs (1993) argued 'an excessive number of national experts, particularly in posts of responsibility, also calls into question the independence of the European civil service itself. If national experts are subsequently appointed through different procedures at various levels, to posts in the Commission's staff, the situation becomes even more ambiguous.' The possible end result of this is a clouding of responsibility and the reduction of the 'Community institutional structure . . . to a centre for the striking of compromises between the Community bureaucracy and national bureaucracies'. Consequently it called for an end to the 'extensive use of detached national experts' and asked the Commission not to 'renationalise the management of certain sectors' (Committee on Institutional Affairs 1993).

The seconded officials are frequently confused, even by those who work within the Commission, with non-statutory agents: officials who are engaged on rather diverse arrangements outside the normal recruitment procedures as 'external resources'. They are termed 'external resources' because they used to be employed outside the normal operating budget of the Commission (Part A for 'administrative expenditure'), and were employed under Part B, for 'operating expenditure' (Strasser 1992). The Committee on Budgets of the European Parliament (1992: ss. 14–16) has complained that the figures on the number of staff concerned here are generally unreliable, and even those which the Commission supplied to the Committee appeared somewhat inconsistent. A 1991 Court of Auditors Decision which questioned the legality of the practice of 'mini-budgets' (paying for items outside the main budget), as well as pressure from the European Parliament, led to a greater account being given of the formerly 'off-line' items, although the Committee on Budgets remained somewhat disappointed in 1994 (Committee on Budgets 1994).

The problem of 'mini-budgets' is a large one and only since the 1993 Budget has a clearer account of the numbers involved become available. Figures in the 1995 Budget show that only three-quarters of grade A posts were filled by establishment staff. The Budget breaks down staff numbers into several elliptically defined functions. Table 3.9 makes clear that the dependence on non-establishment officials is much greater in some areas—social area, internal market, flanking policies (including environment and regional policies)—than others, including horizontal services (mainly administrative services), common policies (including agriculture, fisheries, transport), external relations, and economic development.

We can put a little more flesh on these data by looking at the figures given by the Commission to the European Parliament Budget Committee in 1992. To give an approximate account of the importance of non-establishment officials in the Directorates-General, Table 3.10 shows

TABLE 3.9. *Types of A grade staff in Commission posts, 1995*

Task	% establishment	% external	% seconded*	N
Social area	50.9	40.2	8.9	552
Internal market	65.9	22.2	11.9	1,455
Flanking policies	74.6	17.1	8.3	835
Horizontal services	79.6	12.1	8.3	1,194
Common policies	80.4	12.2	7.4	312
External relations	81.5	11.5	7.0	1,447
Economic development	82.0	10.1	7.9	646
TOTAL	74.1	17.1	8.8	6,441

* All seconded officials treated as A grade.

Source: *Official Journal of the European Communities*, L369, 37 (31 Dec. 1994), 375–89 and 415.

the percentage of the total employees (i.e. A, B, C, and D grades) who are auxiliaries (a relatively small group, see Hay 1989), seconded officials (*experts nationaux detachés—ENDs*), and external resource officials. Given that such non-establishment officials are disproportionately A grade, Table 3.10 is likely to underestimate their significance. Nevertheless, even on this measure there are four DGs (excluding the now defunct DG XXII) where over one-third of officials are non-establishment; in two of them, Enterprise and Environment, over one-half of officials are non-establishment. In only seven Directorates General is the percentage below 10 per cent, with the Personnel Directorate General (DG IX) having the smallest percentage of non-establishment officials. The Commission's Secretariat General and central services tend to have relatively fewer *ENDs* and external resource personnel, with the exception of the Statistical Office with just under one-third non-establishment officials.

7. WORKING IN A MULTINATIONAL BUREAUCRACY

Perhaps the most obvious feature of a multinational bureaucracy is the amount of resources devoted to translating and interpreting between one

TABLE 3.10. *Non-establishment Commission officials, by Directorate General, 1992*

Organization	Establishment officials	Auxiliary officials	Seconded officials	External resource officials	Total, all types officials	% non-establishment officials
DG XXIII Enterprise	67	3	7	144	221	69.7
DG XI Environment	161	4	19	152	336	52.1
DG XXII Cohesion (defunct)	60	2	8	47	117	48.7
DG V Employment, Social Affairs	344	4	28	260	636	45.9
Task Force Educ., Training, Youth	70	4	9	38	121	42.1
DG XII Science	611	0	3	360	974	37.3
Statistical Office	364	1	10	160	535	32.0
DG XIII Telecommunications	641	0	7	292	940	31.8
DG XVI Regional	246	12	28	50	336	26.8
DG I External Relations	753	13	51	202	1,019	26.1
DG III Industry	439	1	13	135	588	25.3
DG XXI Customs	232	5	29	24	290	20.0
DG XVII Energy	432	6	6	83	527	18.0
DG X Audiovisual	397	6	5	65	473	16.1
DG VII Transport	137	6	10	9	162	15.4
DG VI Agriculture	789	11	54	48	902	12.5
DG XIV Fisheries	164	6	5	9	184	10.9
DG XV Internal Market	92	3	7	1	103	10.7

TABLE 3.10. *(cont.)*

Organization	Establishment officials	Auxiliary officials	Seconded officials	External resource officials	Total, all types officials	% non-establishment officials
DG IV Competition	339	3	25	9	376	9.8
DG XX Financial Control	168	6	10	0	184	8.7
DG XIX Budgets	255	20	4	0	279	8.6
Secretariat General	442	11	6	19	478	7.5
DG VIII Development	713	9	12	33	767	7.0
DG II Econ. and Finance	242	7	7	2	258	6.2
Legal Service	173	5	6	0	184	6.0
DG XVIII Credits	100	4	2	0	106	5.7
DG IX Personnel	2,547	61	8	0	2,616	2.6
Joint Interpreting Service	462	4	0	0	466	0.9
Translation Service	1,619	9	0	0	1,628	0.6
Other	180	5	5	40	230	21.7
TOTAL	13,239	231	384	2,179	16,033	17.4

Source: Committee on Budgets (1992).

TABLE 3.11. *Language (LA) staff in European Union institutions, 1995*

	N	% of all staff	Ratio LA to A grade staff
Economic and Social Committee	119	23.4	2.1
Council	490	21.3	1.8
European Court of Justice	224	26.8	1.5
Parliament	679	18.0	1.3
Commission (excluding research centres)	1,644	11.0	0.4
Court of Auditors	49	11.5	0.3
TOTAL	3,205	13.3	0.6

Source: *Official Journal of the European Communities*, L369, 37 (31 Dec. 1994), 154–77.

language and another. Approximately one in seven European Union officials is an LA grade employee, that is, employed in translating and interpreting. The complement of language and translation staff is proportionately greatest in the Economic and Social Committee where the LA grade staff compose nearly one-quarter of all employees and outnumber grade A employees (who are paid at the same rate as LA graders) by 2 : 1 (Table 3.11). In the Council and the European Court of Justice the presence of language workers is also strong by these two measures; there are relatively far fewer in the Commission (11.0 per cent or 0.4 for every grade A worker) and the Court of Auditors (11.5 per cent and 0.3).

Hay (1989: 23) suggests that simply adding up the translation staff 'seriously underestimates those engaged on language work because in all the services many officials undertake some translation and much typing of different language versions of texts'. Hay estimated in 1989 that this group totalled around 500. However, one could go further and argue that almost all senior officials to some degree are engaged in language work. It would be mistaken to see the use of many different languages being entirely covered by the translating and interpreting staff. Senior officials rarely rely upon translators or interpreters for their daily work. Most expect to deal in a language other than their native tongue every day.

TABLE 3.12. *Average claimed number of languages spoken by senior EU officials (all institutions)*

Nationality	Average number claimed	N
Portuguese	4.8	47
Spanish	4.8	74
Dutch	4.8	41
Belgian	4.7	78
German	4.5	114
Luxembourgeois	4.5	14
Italian	4.4	110
Greek	4.3	42
Danish	4.2	40
UK	3.8	148
Irish	3.6	27
French	3.5	123

Sources: *The European Companion* (1992, 1993); *Euro Who's Who* (1991).

Of the 862 officials in all institutions about whom information was available on this topic, only 2.7 per cent claimed to be unable to speak or write any language other than their own (Table 3.12). The average number of languages spoken by officials (including their native tongue) was 4.2. Parachuted officials were less multilingual (average number of languages claimed 4.1) than non-parachuted officials (4.6). Directors General in the Commission are likely to speak fewer languages (3.9) than other senior officials. However, a larger source of variation is the nationality of the official. The Portuguese, Spanish, Dutch, and Belgians appear the most multilingual, speaking an average of 4.8 languages. The French (3.5) claim to speak the fewest languages followed by the Irish (3.6) and the British (3.8). The British, Irish, and French need not worry about their more modest language skills since almost all senior officials speak French or English: 98.3 per cent of all officials and even 97.8 per cent of officials who do not have it as a mother tongue speak English; the figures for French are 97.3 per cent and 93.4 per cent respectively. German, Italian, and Spanish are claimed by around one-half of non-native officials, while one-third or less non-native speakers speak the remaining languages (Table 3.13).

TABLE 3.13. *Languages spoken by officials*

Language	N of officials speaking language	%	% non-native speakers
English	845	98.3	97.8
French	837	97.3	96.4
German	514	59.8	53.6
Italian	445	51.7	44.7
Spanish	419	48.7	43.9
Dutch	242	28.1	17.4
Portuguese	162	18.8	14.1
Danish	80	9.3	4.9
Greek	53	6.2	1.3
Regional	22	2.6	0.0
Gaelic	15	1.7	0.0

Sources: *The European Companion* (1992, 1993); *Euro Who's Who* (1991).

8. CONCLUSIONS: COHESION AND DIVERSITY IN THE EUROPEAN UNION

These two chapters set out to explore the degree to which the civil service of the European Union could be said to be cohesive. The hopes of Jean Monnet were that the European civil service would be a lean, energizing force within Europe. While the numbers of officials exceeded Monnet's notional maximum on the day the European Coal and Steel Community opened for business, the patterns of differentiation within the EU civil service have less to do with number of officials employed within them than with the nature of the institutions of the European Union.

As Spierenberg identified, it is extraordinarily difficult to do much about the organization of the EU administration, whether at the level of the section, directorate, or directorate general, because of the acute sensitivity of the organization to the interests or pride of member states. While it would be mistaken to regard the structure as unchanging, except for additional units being created as new members join, the scope for manœuvre is limited; as the creation of new 'agencies' (the European Monetary Institute, Europol, etc. see p. 27) showed, every country wants a piece of the action.

The need to maintain a balance within the EU civil service has created a number of other characteristic divisions within the EU. There is a clear distinction between career officials and those at the top, broadly A3 and above, who have been appointed, whether from the outside or not, according to criteria in which nationality plays a very large part. Appointments at the top are not necessarily made on the basis of a crude 'national flags' type system where posts are 'reserved' for particular nationalities. The nationality issue is at the heart of a more general political process of senior level appointments, involving Council and Commission members. At stake in this process, whether the post is to be filled by parachuting in an outsider or promoting an insider, is not so much whether the post 'belongs' to a particular nationality but whose turn it is to have another of their nationals at this level. This political process and the difficulties it generates has created a number of further divisions within the EU. There is the obvious distinction between the career and political officials. Less often appreciated, but arguably at least as important, are the differences between the establishment permanent officials, those who have joined the EU through the competitive entry examination and pursued a career as EU officials, and the other groups who have not—above all, seconded national officials and 'external resources'. Such non-establishment groups play a large and important role in major segments of European Union administration. On top of the organizational divisions that exist within any bureaucracy (local, national, or international), the multinational status of the EU creates a number of other divisions. The next chapter explores the degree to which, despite differences in status and nationality, EU officials share a distinctive identity in their career, training, and background.

4

People at the Top

1. EU SERVANTS AS A CASTE

In what sense can we think of European civil servants as a distinctive group? We know they are distinctive since they have chosen, most of them, to live outside the country of their birth. The lifestyle of top officials is to some extent similar since they earn similar amounts of money and live in or around Brussels. Many live in the more pleasant suburbs of Brussels, have children going to the European School, spend Sunday afternoons in Bruges, and go skiing in winter. But similar life-styles do not make EU civil servants a distinctive social group.

There are a variety of senses in which studies of civil services have sought to characterize civil servants as forming a distinctive social group. The literature on 'representative bureaucracy' tends to stress the sociological make-up of top officials (see Sheriff 1976). This literature invariably finds that top civil servants come strongly disproportionately from the traditionally advantaged groups within a society: males from middle-class families. Section 2 of this chapter shows that the European Union is no exception to this. However, it is rare for social background alone to have a particularly decisive impact upon the character of the higher civil service. There are exceptions, such as the military character given to the German bureaucracy of the Imperial and to a lesser extent the Weimar periods, deriving from the strong links between military and civil service within the Prussian nobility (see Roehl 1994). The 'clubbish' atmosphere of the higher civil service in Britain derives from an upper middle class culture nurtured in public schools, Oxford, and Cambridge (see Hennessy 1989). Since it recruits from nation states as different as Portugal, Denmark, Belgium, and the United Kingdom, we would look in vain for any such common socialization experiences in the European Union. Any similarities as a social group are more likely to emerge from similar outlooks derived from educational experiences—are top European civil servants a community, or set of communities, of professionals or specialists? This question is examined in the section 3 of this chapter. Finally this chapter goes on to look at whether the career and background patterns serve conversely to reinforce the differences of status and position between career and political or parachuted officials.

2. EU OFFICIALS AS CONVENTIONAL CIVIL SERVANTS

In sociological terms senior officials within the European Union are similar to officials in member states—predominantly male and middle class. We have no direct measure of parental background, but on one measure which serves as a reasonably good proxy for social background, education, top officials are overwhelmingly middle class in origin. While absence of details from the bibliographical sources does not necessarily mean no university education, among those 1,131 for whom most details were available on careers only 1 per cent did not give a university qualification; 32 per cent gave a Bachelors degree as their highest qualification, 37 per cent a Masters degree, and 30 per cent a doctorate. Germans (61 per cent), Dutch (44 per cent), and Greeks (43 per cent) were the most likely nationalities to have doctorates, while Danish (7 per cent), Irish (10 per cent), British (12 per cent), and Portuguese (15 per cent)[1] were among the least likely to have doctorates.

In our sample only 7 per cent of officials are women. This finding is hardly surprising since most studies of senior officials in nation states have found few women in top jobs, political, administrative, or otherwise. In their study using data from Britain, France, Italy, Germany, Netherlands, and the United States in the early 1970s, Aberbach, Putnam, and Rockman (1981: 47) argue 'Males dominate the administrative elites . . . for fewer than 1 per cent of our senior civil servants are female. Women constitute 4 per cent of our supplementary samples of administrative high fliers (especially promising, younger bureaucrats), a finding that perhaps augurs some slight modification of the sexual composition of future administrative elites.' If there has been a modification in national administrative élites it has been slight (Derlien 1990). While systematic, direct comparisons with the contemporary sex

[1] To some extent the holding of a Ph.D. depends upon the status of a Ph.D. in professional careers. In some countries a doctorate is linked almost exclusively to an academic career—as in Portugal where a Ph.D. would not be taken until a relatively late stage in an academic career—while in others, such as Germany and the Netherlands it is not.

TABLE 4.1. *Women in European administration: senior officials, all institutions*

Institution	% women	N men and women
ESC	12	49
Parliament	11	176
Commission	8	1,423
Translating and interpreting	22	36
Other Central Services	16	198
DGs and Secretariat General	6	915
Commission agencies	5	83
External representation	5	123
Permanent Representations	6	218
Courts	5	62
EIB	4	141
Council	3	116
Court of Auditors	2	42
TOTAL	7	2,227

Sources: *The European Companion* (1992, 1993); *Euro Who's Who* (1991).

composition of administrative élites of member states are difficult because national statistics have very different seniority grades, the evidence does not suggest the EU is much different from member states in the 1990s. One indicator of this similarity between the EU and member states is that the permanent representations of member states contain just 6 per cent women (Table 4.1).

Moreover, women are generally restricted to the less decisive policy-making positions within the EU service. Women are best represented in two smaller institutions—the Economic and Social Committee and the Secretariat of the European Parliament (12 per cent and 11 per cent respectively), less well represented in the Courts of Justice and First Instance (5 per cent), the European Investment Bank (4 per cent), the Council (3 per cent), and the Court of Auditors (2 per cent). In the Commission as a whole, including agency staffs, officials working in member states as well as the Brussels staff of the DGs and its services, 8 per cent of employees in senior positions are women. In the centres of administrative power of the Commission's DGs and Secretariat General women constitute 6 per cent of senior officials. In the central

TABLE 4.2. *Women in senior Commission posts*

Grade	% women	N men and women
A1	3	41
A2	2	185
A3	9	841
A4 and below	17	209
Others	6	147
TOTAL	8	1,423

Sources: *The European Companion* (1992, 1993); *Euro Who's Who* (1991).

services of the Commission, women are most represented in the translation and interpreting services (22 per cent)—in the Translation Service, 28 per cent of senior officials are women.

The lower status given to women is reinforced by the fact that the lower down in the hierarchy one descends, the higher the proportion of women. Taking the Commission alone, women constitute little over 2 per cent of the top grades of A1 and A2; in grades A4 and below they account for 16 per cent (Table 4.2). The figures are too small to make any reliable inferences about national differences in the number of women in top EU positions; larger countries, with the apparent exception of Germany, tend to have more women in senior positions (Table 4.3), but overall the relatively small variation in national proportions served to highlight the absence of large numbers of women from top jobs in the EU. The system of parachuting, which has the potential to compensate to some degree for sex bias in recruitment and promotion within the European Union has not generally had this effect. Commissioners themselves have been overwhelmingly men (of all commissioners between 1967 and 1994 only two were women, in the 1995 Santer Commission there are four). Moreover, while the numbers are very small, parachuting seems no more likely to favour women than working through the ranks—the proportion of women is marginally lower (4 per cent) among parachutists in the Commission Secretariat General and DGs than among career officials (4.8 per cent).

Senior officials of the European Union are generally around the same age as their counterparts in member states. The available evidence for member states is very dated. Aberbach, Putnam, and Rockman (1981:

TABLE 4.3. *Nationality of women in senior posts in Commission Directorates General and Secretariat General*

Nationality	N of women	% of nationality
Belgian	3	5
Danish	0	0
Dutch	1	3
French	7	6
German	0	0
Greek	2	6
Irish	0	0
Italian	9	7
Luxembourgeois	1	8
Portuguese	0	0
Spanish	0	0
UK	5	5

Sources: *The European Companion* (1992, 1993); *Euro Who's Who* (1991).

TABLE 4.4. *Average age of top EU officials, 1993*

Institution	Average age	Standard deviation	N of cases
Commission	53.9	6.9	762
Council	53.6	9.0	67
Parliament	52.0	6.9	94
Perm. Reps.	46.7	8.9	129
Auditors	57.1	8.3	28
Courts	55.6	8.2	49
EIB	53.9	7.4	99
ESC	53.0	6.9	32

Sources: *The European Companion* (1992, 1993); *Euro Who's Who* (1991).

69) give the age of the 'average senior civil servant' in the early 1970s as 53. This figure is close to the average age of the senior officials in the Commission (53.9), Council (53.6), Parliament (52.0), EIB (53.9), Economic and Social Committee (53.0). Only officials in the Courts (55.6) and Court of Auditors (57.1) are appreciably above 53 years old (Table 4.4).

TABLE 4.5. *Age of entry of Commission officials*

Age	A1	A2	A3	A4 and below	Other
29 and under	20.6	31.7	30.0	36.8	22.2
30 to 39	29.4	34.9	45.5	42.1	54.3
40 to 49	47.1	26.2	18.4	21.1	19.8
50 and over	2.9	7.1	6.1	0	3.7

Sources: *The European Companion* (1992, 1993); *Euro Who's Who* (1991).

Given the importance of length of service in promotion in member-state bureaucracies, it may be at first surprising that length of service appears to play a smaller role in the higher reaches of the European Union since the age of officials does not vary particularly strongly between grades. In the Commission the average age of a grade A1 officials is 56.13 years, A2 is 55.38, grade A3 53.86, and A4 52.36. This finding supports a common complaint among unions and staff associations that there are large numbers of older officials stuck at the level above which political contacts are required for promotion (see Rotacher and Colling 1987). The average age of officials from the newer member states tends to be younger than that of longer established members of the European Union, especially officials from Greece (average age 50.2 years), Portugal (47.7), and Spain (48.6). This lower average for these nationalities is generally maintained across the EU institutions and at all levels of seniority in our data set.

3. EDUCATIONAL AND PROFESSIONAL BACKGROUND

Many officials join the EU service later in their careers. With very little variation among different EU institutions, or even different parts of the Commission (whether one looks at officials in DGs, central services, or agencies), most begin their careers outside the institutions of the EU. Of the 1,127 officials on which there is sufficient information, 292 or 26 per cent, had the EU as their first major job, defined as having been occupied before the age of 30; 74 per cent have had previous occupations. We can estimate from the age of entry that between two-thirds (the figure for A4–8 officials—see Table 4.5) and four-fifths (the figure for A1 officials) entered the EU after the age of 30 and might thus be expected to have at least begun a career outside it.

The most common previous occupation held by officials is that of civil servant—45 per cent of officials in all institutions who had careers before joining the EU were formerly civil servants. Officials in the Council Secretariat (59 per cent), the Court of Auditors (62 per cent), and the Court of Justice and Court of First Instance (65 per cent) are more likely to have been civil servants than those in the Commission agencies (18 per cent). The Commission agencies are dominated by research institutes such as the Joint Research Centre where the majority of top officials giving a previous occupation (71 per cent) had held posts in educational institutions before going to the EU. As one would expect, education and the free professions are relatively well represented in the Courts (37 per cent compared with the service average of 12 per cent). The other large group are those who were employed in educational institutions (35 per cent).

The educational backgrounds of top officials is diverse. Overall, officials tend to have social-science or law degrees. There is some tendency for European officials to reflect national traditions in training top officials. Officials from the United Kingdom and the Republic of Ireland are far more likely to provide humanities or arts-educated candidates for top official positions (55.7 per cent and 48.6 per cent respectively) than any other country—the closest to the British Isles overrepresentation of arts graduates is found in Luxembourg (15 per cent). Among the eighty-four top British EU officials in the Commission DGs and Central Services on whom there was sufficient educational background information, thirty-eight or 45.2 per cent had degrees from Oxford or Cambridge—again this overrepresentation reflects the dominance of these two universities in providing senior officials within the United Kingdom civil service. The recruitment of lawyers also reflects known tendencies within national bureaucracies; in the heartland of the European Union the traditional link between law and bureaucracy established at the national level is replicated at the EU level (49.1 per cent of Germans, 43.9 per cent of Italians, 43.3 per cent of Dutch, and 43.5 per cent of French), while this is weaker in the southern edges (Greece and Portugal 36.8 and 36.7 per cent respectively, Spain 34.7 per cent) and even weaker on the western and northern edges (UK 12.4 per cent, Republic of Ireland 18.9 per cent, and Denmark 28.1 per cent).

While there used to be much discussion about the degree of 'specialization' within bureaucracies, it is impossible to determine this simply

TABLE 4.6. *Previous occupations of EU officials (% multiple responses coded)*

	All institutions	Comm. DGs, SG	Comm. services	Comm. agencies	Comm. Dip. rep.	Council Sec.	Ct. Aud.	Eur. Cts.	EIB	EP Sec.	ESC	Other
Civil service	45	43	41	18	43	59	62	65	50	30	33	73
Free professions	12	10	17	2	11	13	14	37	6	20	0	8
Education	35	34	45	71	24	26	10	48	23	30	58	32
Interest groups	1	1	1	4	2	2	0	2	2	0	4	0
Policy advice	7	6	5	0	11	6	14	11	6	10	4	11
Politics	4	3	0	0	6	0	19	7	1	13	4	5
Journalism	5	4	4	0	20	3	5	0	0	22	8	0
Private sector	32	35	28	29	30	28	38	9	54	20	29	8
Public sector	3	0	0	0	0	2	0	0	0	2	0	0
N	913	400	78	45	54	53	21	46	95	60	24	37

Note: Comm. = Commission, SG = Secretariat General, Ct. Aud. = Court of Auditors, EIB = European Investment Bank, EP = European Parliament, ESC = Economic and Social Committee.

Sources: *The European Companion* (1992, 1993); *Euro Who's Who* (1991).

TABLE 4.7. *Educational background of EU officials (% multiple responses coded)*

	UK	IRL	L	NL	F	D	DK	B	GR	E	I	P	All
Arts, Languages, and Humanities	55.7	48.6	15.0	14.9	13.1	12.9	12.3	10.7	7.0	6.3	5.2	5.0	18.3
Social Sciences	34.6	51.4	55.0	46.3	57.6	44.8	57.9	55.4	54.4	62.1	46.5	48.3	49.6
Law	12.4	18.9	50.0	43.3	43.5	49.1	28.1	40.5	36.8	34.7	43.9	36.7	36.5
Natural Sciences	23.8	13.5	15.0	13.4	32.5	18.4	21.1	27.3	43.9	31.6	23.2	23.3	25.1
N	185	37	20	67	191	163	57	121	57	95	155	60	1,208

Sources: *The European Companion* (1992, 1993); *Euro Who's Who* (1991).

TABLE 4.8. *Concentration of different forms of academic specialization in EU organizations*

	Social sciences	Law	Arts	Natural sciences
Mean	52.5	36.6	15.0	25.3
Standard deviation	18.7	19.3	11.3	24.2
Coefficient of variability	0.36	0.53	0.75	0.95

N = 34 organizations.

Sources: *The European Companion* (1992, 1993); *Euro Who's Who* (1991).

from the educational backgrounds of officials—a nuclear physicist would not be a specialist were he or she placed in an organization responsible for regulating competition. Thus simply knowing that the European Union is dominated by lawyers and social scientists, with significant numbers of natural scientists, does not tell us about their deployment. The academic disciplines spread most evenly across thirty-four organizational sections of the EU[2] (as measured by the ratio of the standard deviation to the mean also known as the coefficient of variability) throughout the organizations of the EU administration are the social sciences (0.36—see Table 4.8) and law (0.53). Natural scientists seem to be concentrated in particular organizations since the coefficient of variation is high (0.95). Arts graduates too (0.75) tend to be concentrated in particular organizations.

Some indication of where these officials are concentrated can be seen in Table 4.9, which tends to confirm common-sense assumptions. The natural scientists are concentrated in the Commission agencies (dominated by the research centres), DG XII (Science, Research and Development), and DG XIII (Telecommunications, Information, Market and Exploitation of Research). Arts graduates are not nearly as numerous as the other three groups, and they tend to be relatively concentrated in the servicing of the Commission, the Parliament, and the Council. Law graduates predominate in the courts as well as the more law-intensive

[2] Of these, 27 are within the Commission (the 23 DGs, including the now defunct DG XXII, the secretariat of the Commission, the central services of the Commission, the diplomatic representation of the Commission, and the agencies of the Commission (dominated by the scientific research centres) plus the Courts, the Parliament Secretariat, the EIB, the Court of Auditors, the Economic and Social Committee, the Council Secretariat, and a small 'other' category.

TABLE 4.9. *Organizations containing highest concentrations of officials with academic qualifications in different subjects*

Subject of degree	Institution	%	N
Law	Courts	93.8	48
	DG IV Competition	66.7	18
	DG V Employment	52.9	17
	DG X Audiovisual	50.0	16
	Auditors	48.0	25
Social Science	DG II Ec. and Fin.	85.0	20
	DG XVI Regional	71.4	14
	Ec. and Soc. C'ttee	70.4	27
	DG XIV Fisheries	70.0	10
	DG III Industry	68.8	32
Arts	Commission Sec. Gen.	25.9	27
	Parliament Secretariat	25.6	86
	Council Secretariat General	23.0	61
	DG XVII Energy	22.7	22
	Commission Services	21.7	92
Natural Science	DG XII Science, Research	88.1	42
	Commission Agencies	84.0	50
	DG XIII Telecoms.	81.4	43
	DG XI Env., Nuclear Safety	61.5	13
	DG VII Transport	50.0	10

Sources: *The European Companion* (1992, 1993); *Euro Who's Who* (1991).

DG IX responsible for Competition. Social-science graduates are predominant in DG II Economics and Finance, the Economic and Social Committee, and DG III Industry. Social-science graduates are the most evenly spread throughout the different organizations of the EU.

In the Commission the more traditional qualifications of bureaucrats (arts qualifications in Britain and Ireland, law in Germany, the Netherlands, and Italy and the social sciences in much of Europe) are more likely to be found among the more senior officials because the more senior the official the less likely he or she is to have a natural-science degree (Table 4.10). At the A3 level natural scientists outnumber arts and humanities graduates by over three to one. This ratio drops to two to one at the A2 level, and among A1 officials there are fewer natural scientists than arts and humanities graduates.

TABLE 4.10. *Educational background by grade (Directorates General and Secretariat General only)*

	Arts	Social Sciences	Law	Natural Sciences	N
A1	14.0	44.2	32.6	9.3	43
A2	10.3	42.1	29.4	18.3	126
A3	8.7	38.6	23.3	29.4	391
A4 and below	8.1	33.9	27.4	30.6	62
All	9.3	39.2	25.6	25.9	622

Sources: *The European Companion* (1992, 1993); *Euro Who's Who* (1991).

4. POLITICAL AND CAREER OFFICIALS

So far little evidence has been unearthed to suggest that the EU civil service is a distinctive social group. Like most senior civil servants in all developed nations they are male and come from middle-class homes. Their education is likely to be in the social sciences, but there is some reflection of national bureaucratic profiles—the German lawyer and the British arts graduate—within the European service. However, we have been considering the European Union civil service as a whole. A large number of commentators point to one basic distinction among top officials: between the career officials and those who are appointed to top positions because their appointment was championed by a commissioner or by member states through permanent representatives or the Council of Ministers. The two most frequently cited methods of 'political' promotion are through parachuting (see Chapter 3) and through the practice of joining a commissioner's *cabinet*, the body of advisers with which the commissioner surrounds himself (see Chapter 6). Through membership of a *cabinet* it is possible for a career official to develop closer contacts with the political networks within the European Union and launch himself or herself into a political career.

Despite the obvious outward signs of political appointment, it is impossible to determine who is a 'political appointee' in this sense. Appointments to the level of A3 and above routinely involve the approval of commissioners, and thus to some degree all senior appointments can be termed political. While, as we have seen in Chapter 3, parachutists (those who have been appointed directly to a senior EU position from outside) are generally considered political appointees, it

TABLE 4.11. *Percentage of civil servants with political careers (all institutions)*

	Have been in cabinet		
	Yes	No	TOTAL
Parachuted	8	49	57
Not parachuted	4	38	42
TOTAL	12	87	99*

(N = 1,174)

* Percentages add up to less than 100 due to rounding.

Sources: *The European Companion* (1992, 1993); *Euro Who's Who* (1991).

is possible for career officials to be politically promoted. Thus we must be somewhat cautious when relying upon the main outward signs of political appointment: being parachuted and joining a commissioner's cabinet.

The *cabinet* can be an important means of political promotion. Certainly many officials believe it to be. A Commission survey found that over 40 per cent of grade A3–5 officials felt that you needed to have 'served some time in one of the members' *cabinets*' to get on in the Commission, compared with under 20 per cent believing that you needed to 'produce results' (European Commission 1988). However, the number of officials who follow this path to high administrative office is relatively small. Within the EU as a whole, the bulk of top officials, 87 per cent, have not been members of a commissioner's *cabinet.* Almost a half (49 per cent) are simple parachutists (see Table 4.11), whereas well over one-third (38 per cent) are career officials who have not been members of a *cabinet.* There is, however a clear relationship between membership of a *cabinet* and seniority in the EU administration; 32 per cent of A1 and A2 officials have been members of a *cabinet* compared with 12 per cent for grade A3 and below. Not only are the numbers of top officials who have been cabinet members small, but most of them (two-thirds of the 12 per cent who had been in *cabinets*) were parachutists. The career European civil servant who uses membership of a *cabinet* to switch from a routine administrative career to join the higher reaches of the service consists of 10 per cent of grades A1 and A2 but only 4 per cent of top civil servants overall. Even at the top two levels these

TABLE 4.12. *Parachutists from different member states*

	% in all institutions	% in Commission*	N officials in all institutions
Spain	93.5	94.3	93
Portugal	89.5	100.0	57
Ireland	75.7	68.8	37
Greece	73.7	75.0	57
Denmark	73.6	73.3	53
United Kingdom	65.2	61.0	198
Netherlands	63.1	70.8	65
Luxembourg	57.1	50.0	21
Germany	49.7	42.9	159
Belgium	45.7	33.3	116
France	44.3	33.7	185
Italy	35.1	29.9	151
All member states	58.4	51.4	1,192

* Secretariat General and Directorates General only.

Sources: *The European Companion* (1992, 1993); *Euro Who's Who* (1991).

officials are outnumbered two to one by career officials with no obvious political connection either as parachutists or *cabinet* members. Thus in our discussion of political appointments we will concentrate upon the distinction between parachuted and non-parachuted officials.

Parachuting might be associated with the patronage of clientelistic political systems of southern Europe while promotion of serving officials on the basis of merit might be associated with the more rational-bureaucratic systems of northern Europe. However, such a view is not supported by the evidence. Table 4.12 shows that parachuting is largely unrelated to what are generally considered to be the major features of national bureaucratic cultures. Italy, where clientelism is commonly believed to pervade the political system, is among the least likely to parachute officials. The Netherlands, where the decline of pillarization since the 1960s has decreased the role of party patronage in the bureaucracy, is one of the most likely to parachute officials. Table 4.12 suggests a somewhat simpler reason to explain national differences in parachuting. The degree to which European officials from any one member state are parachuted in to the EU civil service to a large extent

TABLE 4.13. *Years of service of officials in Secretariat General and Directorates General, 1993*

Years	% career	% parachuted
0–5	1	23
6–10	3	20
11–15	15	13
Over 15	81	43
Total N	234	230

Sources: *The European Companion* (1992, 1993); *Euro Who's Who* (1991).

depends upon the date at which the country joined the EU. For the older member states there is a greater chance of recruiting top officials from among career officials who have served the EU for many years. Among officials in all institutions the newer members—Spain, Portugal, Greece—are among those with the highest proportion of parachutists, whereas the older members have the lowest (see Table 4.12). A similar pattern emerges if one considers the officials in the Commission's Directorates General and Secretariat General only.

One must also guard against viewing parachutists as troubleshooters brought in to do a specific job for their home governments, with them resuming their domestic tasks when it is done. Such a view of political appointees can be found in the 'in and outer' system as it was widely considered to operate in the United States (but see Heclo 1988). Under such a system political appointment to serve within the bureaucracy is a temporary phase in the career of an individual; the appointee enters Washington with little previous Washington experience and then returns to the job, probably in a law firm, that he or she occupied before but with enhanced status. In the European Union parachutists tend to stay on once they have been appointed (Table 4.13). Of non-parachuted career officials in our data set, 96 per cent had been in the EU civil service for over ten years in 1993; 56 per cent of parachutists had stayed in the EU administration for over ten years. Moreover, the bulk of parachuted officials in service for less than ten years were from the newer member states: Spain (31 per cent), Portugal (11 per cent), and Greece (13 per cent). In 1993 the average parachuted official had been in the EU service for 14.6 years, while the career official had been in

TABLE 4.14. *Age of entry into EU service of career officials and parachutists*

	Career officials %	Subsequent parachutists %	Parachuted in at start %
29 and below	51	5	12
30–39	46	40	40
40–49	3	36	41
50 and over	0	19	6
N	478	431	218

Sources: *The European Companion* (1992, 1993); *Euro Who's Who* (1991).

it for 24.4 years. While they have served for less time on average than other officials, the evidence suggests that once parachuted in, most of them stay there.

Are parachutists any different from career officials? There are some obvious differences. As they are catapulted from careers elsewhere into high EU positions they are generally likely to have joined the EU much later in their lives. The average age of senior civil servants in all organizations in 1993 was little different for parachutists (52.6 years) than non-parachuted officials (53.7 years), although grade-for-grade parachutists tended to be on average around two years younger than career officials. Yet almost all (97 per cent) career officials joined the EU before their fortieth birthdays, compared with fewer than one-half (45 per cent) of parachutists, leaving aside those who were parachuted during the first two years of their home country joining the European Union. Those parachuted during the early months of their country's EU membership were only slightly younger (52 per cent under 40) than other parachutists.

Since they tended to join the EU civil service later in their lives, the major difference between the professional experience of parachuted and career officials is that just over one-half of career officials, 53.3 per cent, have not had a career outside the European Union.[3] Parachuted officials above all (62.1 per cent) are more likely to have been previously employed in national civil service than career officials (14.4 per cent—Table 4.15). Of those parachuted in from national civil services

[3] Those on whom there is no other information and who joined the EU before the age of 30 have been classified as having no previous major profession.

TABLE 4.15. *Previous occupation(s) of EU officials*

	Parachutists %	Career officials %	Overall %
Civil servant	62.1	14.4	42.2
Professional occupations	10.3	6.3	8.6
Education	28.9	18.8	24.7
Interest group	1.4	0.7	1.1
Policy advice	9.0	1.1	5.7
Politics	4.8	0.2	2.9
Journalism	4.8	3.1	4.1
Private sector	27.0	15.7	22.3
Public enterprises	0.3	0	0.2
No previous occupation	0	53.3	22.2
N	641	458	1,099

Sources: *The European Companion* (1992, 1993); *Euro Who's Who* (1991).

nearly half (47.1 per cent) had diplomatic experience, compared with just over a quarter (27 per cent) of career officials who had previously served in a national bureaucracy. Some states are more likely to parachute civil servants into top EU positions than others: 78.9 per cent of Danish parachutists are likely to have been civil servants, as are 70.8 per cent of Portuguese parachutists; Belgium (49 per cent), Luxembourg (44.4 per cent), and Germany (56.7 per cent) have relatively fewer civil servants among parachutists, the remaining nations having between 60 and 67 per cent civil-servant parachutists. Education, which is a previous occupation for 28.9 per cent of parachuted officials and 18.8 per cent of career officials, is especially favoured in Belgium (42.9 per cent of parachutists), and the southern member states (Greece 35.0 per cent, Italy 31.7 per cent, Portugal 33.3 per cent, and Spain 43.4 per cent) but less so in France, Denmark, Ireland, and the United Kingdom, where around 20 per cent of parachuted officials are taken from the world of education. The private sector is a major source of parachuted officials (27.0 per cent) although 15.7 per cent of career officials have also worked in private sector. As one might expect, the proportions who had served as professional policy advisers was somewhat higher (9.0 per cent) among parachutists than career officials (1.1 per cent). Those with previous careers in journalism, politics, interest groups (including trade unions and business associations), and public-sector industries all counted for below 10 per cent of parachuted or career officials.

5. CONCLUSIONS

In many respects EU civil servants as a group are little different from senior civil servants in member states. They are overwhelmingly male and from middle-class backgrounds. They tend to be the same age as those who reach higher positions in national civil services. While there are concentrations of technical expertise in some organizations of the European Union, the senior levels in the main Directorates General tend to have a social-science education, although qualifications are likely to reflect national patterns of bureaucratic education, with, for example, Britain having disproportionately larger numbers of arts graduates and Germany disproportionately larger numbers of lawyers. This distinction between lawyers, social scientists, and arts graduates has been associated with differences in approach to policy-making. Putnam suggests that lawyers are more likely to be 'classical' bureaucrats, by which he means that officials perceive for themselves a limited role in the policy process as executors of decisions, and tend to try to follow formal rules and procedures when they do participate in policy-making. Such perceptions and tendencies are not shared by the more 'political' bureaucrats, often with educational backgrounds in social sciences, who participate in the cut and thrust of politics with greater relish (see Putnam 1973). Such linkages between background and role perceptions remain highly speculative. Moreover, a direct relationship between role perceptions and actual role played cannot be taken for granted. In one of the only systematic attempts to examine the effect of educational background, Christensen's survey of Norwegian civil servants concludes that 'type of higher education is not connected to variations in role orientation in Norway' (1991: 309). Like top officials in European nation states, senior officials in the European Union are disproportionately male and middle class. But neither their demographic nor their educational backgrounds constitute characteristics of a distinctive social caste.

One reason which may explain why the characteristics of senior EU officials are similar to those of member-state bureaucrats is that many EU officials were in fact civil servants before they joined the EU service. Of these a large proportion were diplomats. One commentator has suggested that diplomats are more likely than others to 'go native and end up being more understanding of the positions of other member states than of their own' (Hayes-Renshaw *et al.* 1989: 128). However, along with conjectures about the impact of educational background on policy-making roles, such hunches have little direct empirical evidence to support them.

One of the most important factors preventing the EU from constituting a distinctive caste is the division between 'political' and 'merit' appointments. Parachutists are in many respects different from those who have progressed through the service to the top. In Chapter 3 we saw that parachutists were slightly less likely to be multilingual than EU career officials. They tend to have experience within the bureaucracy of their home state. And their presence has an effect upon the perception of civil servants throughout the EU of the nature of EU service. A survey found one of the biggest differences between the Commission and other organizations which the survey research company CEGOS had analysed was that officials believed to a striking extent that you needed 'the right connections to get on in the Commission' (European Commission 1988). This was especially marked, reaching 50 per cent (compared with just over 10 per cent believing the ability to produce results was the key to advancement) in grades A4–6—i.e. the grades containing those who had reached the top of a normal administrative career and above which 'political' factors of one form or another progressively come into play in the appointments process.

One cannot read the character of a bureaucrat simply from knowing how he or she was educated or what job he or she did before reaching the top of the administrative hierarchy. Nevertheless, educational background is often an important component of the culture of any bureaucracy—the world inhabited by the predominantly Oxbridge-educated British civil servant is very different from that of the French ENA graduate or the German lawyer at the top of a federal ministry. The administration of the EU is a cosmopolitan bureaucratic culture. It has people at the top who have worked through the institutions, those who were parachuted long ago, and those who have just hit the ground. It has people on contracts, secondment as well as national civil servants passing through. There are specialists with natural-science backgrounds who have come into the mainstream world of policy-making in major DGs, as well as civil servants with law, social-science, and arts degrees. Such diversity militates against the development of a common identity. In fact to deal with this diversity officials tend to make many assumptions about each other that emphasize such differences: officials from the 'north' behave differently from those from the 'south' (Abeles *et al.* 1993); political officials are simply reaping the rewards of earlier political loyalties; those on temporary contracts are working for a permanent job and seconded officials are working for their home state. If one were looking for a handy simile for European bureaucratic culture then one might find it among similar blends of cosmopolitan and isolated lifestyles, such as on board a merchant ship. Multinational interpersonal relationships, changing sets of colleagues and superiors, a sense of mission and tradition, a flattening of formal hierarchical positions in the face of pressing exigencies, the periods of exhilarating action becoming idealized as 'moments cut free from the repetitious routines of work' (Lane 1986), are factors characteristic of seafaring life which bear some similarity to the impressions given by officials when reflecting about the nature of serving the European Union their work.

> Antagonisms may be modified by the solidarity of seafaring . . . there is an inconclusiveness as to a clear line on the subject of hierarchy. People reach for an embracing generalisation which is firm, clear and simple. And then modify or withdraw it. For all the bitternesses and all the fears there are also the ambivalences, the ambiguities, the alliances, and it is these that save the ship from social warfare (Lane 1986: 158).

5

Bureaucracy and Interest Groups in the European Union

1. GOVERNMENT–GROUP RELATIONS

Interest groups are a ubiquitous phenomenon in Western democratic systems. Those who point to the increasing importance of interest groups in the European Union often use as evidence the large and growing number of associations which are located in Brussels. Mazey and Richardson (1993: 5–6) illustrate the growing importance of groups by their increasing numbers—from 300 groups in 1970 to 439 by 1980 and 525 in the early 1990s. But this does not, of course, exhaust the scale of interest group activity in Brussels; major national interest groups, such as the German Civil Servants Association (Deutscher Beamtenbund), the British National Farmers Union, or the American Pharmaceutical Manufacturers Association, and large corporations, European as well as non-European, have offices in Brussels. There are an estimated 3,000 professional lobbyists concerned specifically with representing clients within the European Union (Mazey and Richardson 1993: 8); the Commission estimated that there were around 10,000 employees in the early 1990s in the lobby industry in Brussels (McLaughlin and Greenwood 1995: 149). McLaughlin, Jordan, and Maloney (1993) suggest that corporate lobbying by firms is frequently more important than group lobbying. The scale of such lobbying by individual firms is exceptionally hard to assess since those firms that do not have more or less permanent representation in Brussels can travel there. Volkswagen, for example, did not have a Brussels office until the early 1990s, and used to direct its lobbying effort, which included chauffeuring the French chairman of the influential *ad hoc* committee on emissions around Brussels, from its Bonn office. Similarly, individual nationally based interest groups may be represented in Brussels without actually having an office there.

The relationship between bureaucrats and interest groups is among the most important defining features of the character of a bureaucracy, whether it is the aloof claim to disdain 'sectional interests' found among the officials serving the French state (Suleiman 1975), the desire to cultivate good relations with groups, whether sympathetic or hostile to the agency, found among bureau chiefs in the United States (Kaufman 1981: 67–70) or the 'consensus-mongering' characteristic of British civil servants (Headey 1974; Peters 1981; Rose 1981).

Interest groups play an important, though variable, part in every liberal democratic political system (see Hayward 1995 for a comparative discussion), and in this sense the European Union is little different to any national political system. Yet if we look at interest-group theory we might expect interest groups to play a greater role in policy-making in the EU than in most member states. First, the main areas of EU activity include those policy concerns which are traditionally the focus for intensive interest-group activity within member states. As Lowi (1964) has argued, the nature of politics, above all the degree to which there are conflicting groups, dominant groups, or few groups participating in the policy process, is shaped by the particular policy area. The dominant policy concern of the European Union, at least in terms of finance (covering around two-thirds of the total budget of the EU) as well as regulation (see Table 5.3 below) is agriculture, which traditionally generates powerful organizations that often enjoy close relationships with national agricultural ministries. In Britain Smith (1992) shows the strong relationship that has developed between the Ministry of Agriculture, Fisheries and Food and the National Farmers Union; in France Keeler's (1981) work shows that the relationship between the one interest group (of the several major French farmers groups) favoured by the state, the Centre National des Jeunes Agriculteurs, is probably the closest one can find to a 'corporatist' relationship in the French political system. Industrial producer organizations, whether large firms or associations, are crucially affected by other major goals of the European Union—the creation and maintenance of a single market, bringing into existence the conditions for fair competition within it as well as the conditions of work for employees. This numerical dominance of organizations representing industrial interests is indicated by the fact that the European Public Affairs Directory in 1994 had listings for the Brussels offices of 463 trade associations and 305 corporations as well as twenty-four national employers organizations and twenty-nine business-related interest groups (such as the European Business Ethics Network). There were fewer groups representing labour unions

(19), international organizations (97), and other non-business interest groups (90). See also Berger and Skærseth (1994: 31).

A second reason for anticipating the importance of interest groups in the European Union lies in the institutional structure of the European Union. The United States is frequently characterized as a political system in which interest groups have enormous leverage over public policies, over the appointment of personnel in public agencies, and can shape the whole style of politics (Lowi 1969; Heclo 1978). One of the main sources of that leverage is the fragmentation of authority within the political system: the separation of powers between legislative, executive, and judicial branches of government, and the diversity of institutions within each branch in addition to the territorial division of powers between federal, state, and local government. While the division of authority is messy and blurred it is nevertheless real. Interest groups in the United States have many possible points of entry into the political system. While in many West European countries such groups tend to focus attention on the executive, in the United States they may focus attention upon a variety of committees within Congress and on the judiciary as well as on executive agencies. In the European Union there is a similar fragmentation of authority. Most obviously there is the division between the powers of the Commission and the Council. The Commission proposes legislation, uses its own direct powers of subordinate legislation, and enforces regulations either directly or through the courts. The Council is the main legislative body. Both Council and Commission are constrained by the interpretation of European Treaties and legislation by the European Court of Justice. Moreover, a neat separation between the spheres of influence of the Council and Commission is by no means easy. As we have seen in the discussion of the 'renationalization' of the European civil service through secondment, temporary appointments, and the role of national governments in the appointment of top officials, the member-state influence is not limited to the Council but also plays a major role in the supranational Commission. Since the Maastricht Treaty of 1992, the powers of the European Parliament have expanded to such a degree that it is now arguably a far more powerful assembly than can be found in many member states (Church and Phinnemore 1994). With such a fragmentation of authority there is some reason to expect interest groups to have similar multiple entry points to those found in the United States.

But what is the impact of intense interest-group activity for the character of the EU civil service? Interest-group theory is not specific about

TABLE 5.1. *Types of group–bureaucracy relationships*

Number of groups	Scope for non-negotiable policy-making	
	Limited	Extensive
High	Issue networks	Consultative pluralism
Low	Corporatism	Clientela

the relationship between the intensity of group activity and the effect this has on the government agencies with which they interact. Two broad sets of characteristics of the relationship between groups and the governmental organization they seek to influence are generally considered to be of particular importance in characterizing the pattern of group–government relationships. First is the number of relevant interests involved in policy-making: is an agency influenced by a variety of competing groups, or are there somewhat cosier relations between one or two dominant groups and the agency? This dimension is referred to in the review of British literature on group–government relations by Rhodes and Marsh (1992: table 1.1 at p. 14) as a question of numbers of members of a 'policy community'. Here some policy networks have highly restricted memberships, others have large numbers of members, and some change over time from limited to larger numbers of members. The second set of characteristics derives from the degree to which these groups occupy a privileged position within the policy process. At one extreme, such groups may hold a veto power and prevent action in areas where agreement with groups cannot be secured, at the other such groups offer their views but can be disregarded with few obvious political risks. To view this from the government perspective, this dimension refers to the degree to which governments can make issues non-negotiable: how far is it possible for the agency to ignore the suggestions made by the groups with which it interacts?

We may combine these to make four broad types of relationship between the organization and the groups (Table 5.1). The terminology used to describe interest group–government relationships is notoriously hotly contested (Rhodes and Marsh 1992), and consequently the explanations of the terminology are more important than the terminology itself. Moreover, since the two dimensions on which they are based are continua rather than discrete distinctions, relationships are bound in real life to be mixed forms. Of course, some forms of group–government relationships, such as *parentela* relationships where relationships are conducted through the intermediary of political parties, are excluded since they have little obvious relevance for the European Union (LaPalombara 1964). Nevertheless the terms in Table 5.1 are somewhat familiar terms to denote four very different types of relationship *in so far as the bureaucracy is concerned.*

Under *issue networks* a large number of interest groups have significant access to the political system and they become powerful inside players in the policy process. The scope for government making issues non-negotiable with groups is here limited. This does not mean that the agreement of any one group is a *sine qua non* of policy-making but rather that it is difficult for government organizations to make policy without agreement from major groups within the networks. This understanding of the term 'issue networks' gives a greater role to groups in the policy process than other recent definitions (Rhodes and Marsh 1992), yet is close to the picture of the impact of such networks in Washington set out by Heclo (1978: 121), where 'the influence of the policy technicians and their networks permeates everything the White House may want to do'. In Richardson and Jordan's (1979) discussion of Britain in the 1970s, which also presents a picture of government–group relations close to the definition of issue networks given here, bureaucracy itself is possibly little more than another group within these networks. Such a picture suggests a vulnerability of bureaucrats to a great variety of group pressures. Moreover, since the passage of legislation or in fact any authoritative governmental act requires the approval of other bodies, bureaucrats must themselves also exert pressure on these bodies and their status in the policy process comes to resemble that of interest-group activists. Such a fusion between interest-group and bureaucratic roles is highlighted by Heclo's discussion of 'public careerists', people who make careers moving between political, bureaucratic, and group jobs: this system 'penalizes bureaucrats for performing as high civil servants . . . In this American system it is obviously very hard to view the bureaucracy as an autonomous participant in policy making' (Heclo 1984: 22–3).

Under *corporatism*, as under issue networks, interest groups have privileged access to the political system, possibly even a potential veto power, yet because there are few of them the relations between groups and the executive are far more stable. Under true corporatism these relationships are managed and formalized through corporatist deliberative bodies. The broader definition of corporatism used in Table 5.1 would include the kind of stable but also formally unmanaged 'iron triangles' imagery, reflecting a cosy relationship between a congressional committee, a large interest group, and an agency which monopolized policy-making in its own particular area, that was used to describe some policy areas in the United States until the 1960s (for a discussion of the term see Jordan 1981). Under such a system bureaucrats have a much greater role in the policy process since they are more or less equal partners in a limited process of negotiation. Such a model of group–bureaucracy relations appears to have been approximated in Britain in the relationship between the National Farmers Union and the Ministry of Agriculture, Fisheries, and Food for much of the post-war period (Smith 1992).

Consultative pluralism refers to a relationship in which a variety of groups with weak or no potential veto power compete for influence within the executive. The transactions between groups and government are primarily consultation rather than negotiation. Under corporatism negotiations take place between more or less equal partners; under issue networks government officials negotiate with representatives of many groups with whom they compete to exercise influence over the final outcome. Under consultative pluralism the relationship between group and government is highly asymmetrical—the group has to persuade a government agency by argument and information. One approximation of this can be found in British taxation policy (Robinson and Sandford 1983). This gives a potentially strong role to bureaucrats since they represent a major source of professional expertise without any direct competition from organized interests.

Clientela relationships refer, in LaPalombara's (1964: 258) terms, to group–government relationships which are '*structured* rather than *fluid*'. They emerge when a single group 'succeeds in becoming, in the eyes of a given administrative agency, the natural expression and representative of a given social sector which, in turn, constitutes the natural target or reference point for the agency' (LaPalombara 1964: 262). Clientela relationships may differ in the degree to which the administration may maintain its autonomy from its 'clients'. Here I understand it in its weaker variant as similar to consultative pluralism. As in consultative pluralism the civil servant has a substantial degree of autonomy and power in the decision-making process, yet the government may select a few key organizations with which to consult. Perhaps the clearest example of this is Keeler's description of the French Centre National des Jeunes Agriculteurs who were selected by the French Ministry of Agriculture as the major ally in a programme of modernization since it was the only major farmers union that was sympathetic to ministry thinking at the time. Groups under such clientela relationships are just as likely to be pressure*d* groups as pressure groups (Hayward 1986).

2. NUMBER OF GROUPS

It is not possible to give an accurate account of the number of groups that operate at the EU level. It is possible, however, to gain some indication of the level of interest-group activity, and which particular parts of the European Union are the major targets of group activity. Butt Phillip's (1991) directory gives a useful list of the major interest groups organized on a Europe-wide basis which replied to a questionnaire sent out in 1991. Butt Phillip does not give details of the selection of groups included in the survey, and there is no means of determining how exhaustively the universe of groups lobbying the EU has been covered. Yet the information offers an interesting perspective on group–Commission relations since, among other things, most of these groups mentioned which specific parts of the EU they have dealings with. Very few mentioned any other institution of the EU except the Commission. Groups also mentioned particular organizations within the Commission with which they had regular dealings.

From Table 5.2 it can be seen that the largest number of groups (175 or 23.5 per cent of all contacts mentioned) refer to links with DG III, the Directorate General responsible for industry and internal market (in 1991; 'internal market' formed a separate DG in 1993). This is followed by Agriculture (DG VI: 87 groups mentioned it). Following that, a large number of DGs as well as the Consumer Policy Service were mentioned as contacts by between two dozen and four dozen groups. There are some with relatively few groups—DG XVI (Regional Policy, ten mentions), DG II (Economic and Financial Affairs, fifteen mentions) and DG XVII (Energy, nine mentions). The internally oriented DG XIX (Budgets), DG XX (Financial Control), DG XVIII (Credit and Investments), and DG IX (Personnel) have between none and two groups mentioning them as contacts. Somewhat more surprising are the few mentions made of Fisheries (DG XIV, one mention).

To some extent the number of groups reflects the size and range of

TABLE 5.2. *Interest groups and the Commission: contacts and contact points*

Directorate General	N groups	%	Contact points	Group intensity
Consumer Policy Service	40	5.4	13	3.08
DG III Industry	175	23.5	84	2.08
DG XI Environment, Civil Protection	46	6.2	34	1.35
DG XXI Customs and Indirect Taxation	31	4.2	25	1.24
DG XXIII Enterprise Policy and Tourism	38	5.1	33	1.15
DG IV Competition	45	6.0	46	0.98
DG VI Agriculture	87	11.7	89	0.98
DG VII Transport	26	3.5	28	0.93
DG V Employment, Industrial Relations, and Social Affairs	47	6.3	57	0.83
DG X Audiovisual, Communication	22	3.0	38	0.58
DG XV Financial Institutions and Company Law	21	2.8	41	0.51
DG XII Science, Research*	33	4.4	80	0.41
DG XIII Telecommunications	29	3.9	72	0.40
DG VIII Development	27	3.6	77	0.35
DG XVI Regional Policy	10	1.3	32	0.31
DG II Economic and Financial Affairs	15	2.0	62	0.24
DG I External Relations	38	5.1	167	0.23
DG XVII Energy	9	1.2	51	0.18
DG IX Personnel	1	0.1	6	0.17
DG XVIII Credits and Investments	2	0.3	16	0.13
DG XIV Fisheries	1	0.1	35	0.03
DG XIX Budgets	0	0	31	0
DG XX Financial Control	0	0	0	0
DG XXII Cohesion (defunct)	2	0.3	na	na

* Excludes JRC and Research Centres.

Sources: Compiled from Butt Phillip (1991); Eurosources (1994).

activities of the different Directorates General. The Consumer Policy Service has a relatively narrowly defined range of functions within the Commission, which do not embrace even the whole of the consumer-policy sector (Gozens 1992), and only one director. DG III is a larger organization with a wider range of functions and six directorates (in 1991). To account for the imbalances in size and range of functions, and to give some impression of the relative intensity of interest-group activity, the number of times the DG is mentioned by a group is divided by the number of 'contact points' cited by the Commission in a guide for outside groups and individuals (Eurosources 1994): see Table 5.2. Since the data on groups only includes those organized on a Europe-wide basis, and since the 'contact points' (to a large extent, heads of sector and ranks above whose work is not primarily concerned with internal EU affairs) have no official or theoretical status, the figures in Table 5.1 should be treated with some caution as indicators of the relative spread of interest-group activity within the Commission. Table 5.2 suggests that the Consumer Policy Service, with over three groups per contact point, and DG III (Industry and Internal Market), with just over two, are among the most extensively lobbied parts of the Commission. Environment, Customs, and Enterprise and Tourism have somewhat over one per contact point, while Competition, Agriculture, Transport and Employment, Industrial Relations and Social Affairs have just under one. In the remaining DGs interest-group contacts are much sparser with fewer than half as many groups as contact points.

What does this pattern tell us about the nature of group–Commission relations (set out in Table 5.1)? The number of groups distinguishes between the corporatist or clientelistic pattern on the one hand and the issue network or consultative pluralistic model on the other. Overall the large number of groups within the EU suggests that taking the EU as a whole we are more likely to find relationships resembling consultative pluralism or issue networks. Yet if we divide up the different parts of the EU the number of groups interacting with different Directorates General varies quite substantially from the extremely sparse (including Fisheries)—suggesting the possibility of clientela or corporatist relations—to the extremely dense (including Industry, Internal Market, and the Consumer Policy Service)—suggesting consultative pluralism or issue network relationships. Nevertheless, of the major externally oriented DGs, only Fisheries appears on the basis of the limited available data to come close to the clientela/corporatist relationship, but we shall see shortly that such a conclusion would be erroneous.

3. THE VETO POWER OF GROUPS

The typology set out in Table 5.1 has as one of its dimensions the number of groups. The actual number of groups in existence is of less relevance to this model than the number of groups having an impact upon policy-making and the strength of that influence. To a large extent the influence that any group can have upon EU policy through lobbying within the Commission depends upon the degree to which the Commission actually makes policy. There are two main ways in which we might look at the Commission's role in policy-making from the perspective of the interest group. First there is the role of the Commission as the proposer of EU legislation, a role given to it in the Treaty of Rome. On this basis group influence within the Commission can be that of initiative—starting the procedures of decision-making, involving dialogue with the European Parliament, Council, and a myriad formal and informal groups and having the ear of the person who writes the all-important first draft of a piece of legislation. Second, there is the extensive scope within the Commission for making policy through powers conferred on it, including, above all, the power to make legislation through Commission regulations and decisions.

3a. The Commission as policy initiator

The majority of European Union legislation (71 per cent—see Table 5.3 below) is Commission legislation. Between 1980 and 1994 there were 918 Council *directives* and 6,108 Council *regulations*. These items of legislation resulted from proposals submitted by the Commission, although a substantial proportion, 19 per cent, of the 1,941 Council *decisions* did not result directly from Commission proposals (to a large extent this 19 per cent comprises measures relating to internal Council procedures).[1] We have no systematic information, or even anecdotal information, about the success rates of Commission proposals. Certainly one can check to see how many Commission proposals for Council legislation actually appear as law in the *Official Journal.* Some indicator of this can be given by the fact that on average over the period 1985–94 the Commission submitted proposals for 414 Council regulations, 112 Council decisions, and 101 Council directives each year. The

[1] The data used in this paragraph was derived from the Celex data base on the Justis CD-Rom.

Council passed 419 regulations and 138 decisions each year, suggesting that virtually all Commission-proposed regulations and decisions become law (although, as we have seen, some decisions are not the result of Commission initiatives). The success rate for Commission proposals for Council directives appears to be lower on this measure. On average 101 Council directives were proposed, but only sixty-nine were passed. This lower success rate is not least because many proposed Council directives (89 per cent) had an additional hurdle of being discussed both in the European Parliament and the Economic and Social Committee, compared with 33 per cent of proposed Council decisions and 31 per cent of proposed Council regulations.

Such figures, however, seriously overestimate the success rate of the Commission in the passage of legislation. These calculations cannot take account of major changes made to proposed legislation before it is actually passed by the Council. Moreover, by the time any initiative actually appears as a proposal in a COM document and is published by the Commission, it has usually been squared with potential opponents and thus has a good chance of becoming a Council regulation, directive, or decision. We have no way of knowing how many proposals are abandoned before they ever appear in publicly available documents. Nor is it possible to determine whether Commission proposals were initiated at the suggestion of the Council. Consequently it is hazardous to take the publication of COM documents as an indicator of policy *initiation* by the Commission (see Sloot and Verschuren 1990). Nevertheless, we must regard the role of the Commission as crucial in the initiation of European Union policy, whether this refers to major matters such as the creation of a single market, a common currency, the reform of the Common Fisheries Policy or the less spectacular basic prices of aubergines.

In this form of Commission activity we would not expect to be able to find any corporatist relationship between any large groups and the Commission since the Commission, though influential, is dependent upon Council approval as well as, under some circumstances, that of other institutions. Council members, as members of national governments, are likely to be the target of domestic, national group pressures exercised directly as well as indirectly through the permanent representatives of member states in Brussels, as well as through the host of domestic civil servants and advisers who participate in the statutory and *ad hoc* advisory bodies set up to consider legislation. The statutory bodies are well documented (see below), in the initiation of legislation the working parties and *ad hoc* groups are somewhat more important since they are a forum for consultation, negotiation, and bargaining between member states. We know relatively little about such groups. Bunyan (1993: 185) allows us to give some illustration of the regularity of such meetings: in the two years 1991 and 1992 there was a total of 227 meetings of *ad hoc* groups and working parties on immigration, crime, and policing. Given the multiple arenas in which EU decisions are made, the chances of any one or a handful of groups organized at the European level having a stable position as a key influence across all institutions on EU policy, even in one particular policy field, are small.

If we take the case of fisheries, an area of policy where EU decisions have a major effect upon a significant sector of the economies of many member states, Butt Phillip (1991) notes only one major Europe-wide interest group (see Table 5.2), Europêche (Association of National Organizations of Fishing Enterprises in the European Union). Yet here we can see not only that the relationship is far from corporatist, but that the pattern of interest-group activity reveals major (national) divisions among fishing interests, and the impact of these interests relies crucially on the degree to which they are successfully represented by national governments within the Council of Ministers, permanent representatives, and officials in the working groups considering EU policy (see p. 106 below).

Despite inclusion in the Treaty of Rome, the initial impetus to create an EEC fisheries policy, it was not until the late 1960s that the Commission began to consider proposing a policy of equal access to all fishing grounds among member states which eventually was set out in a Council regulation (no. 2141) in 1970. The stimulus for this regulation was not pressure from fishing industries or even the national interests of the six members faced with the accession of three major fishing nations to the EEC (Britain, Ireland, and Denmark, with Norway a possible fourth), but as Song (1995: 46) suggests, a more abstract 'legal political necessity to apply the basic EEC principle of nondiscrimination to the fishing sector'. Song goes on to argue that it was only after the initial moves towards a common fisheries policy that the original member states, above all Germany and France, recognized the potential for expanding the fishing grounds of their fleets. Later on, the expansion of the EEC into a larger fisheries management role after the mid-1970s resulted in part from the EEC's extension of its waters to 200 miles, itself a response to the identical actions of Canada, Iceland, Norway, and the United States. This gave rise to protracted negotiations within the

Community, lasting from 1976 to 1983 when a series of Council Regulations were passed (170 and 172 above all) setting out regulations governing net sizes, fishing quotas, and other fisheries-management instruments. In these negotiations, as well as in the negotiations that led to a reformulation of fisheries policy in the early 1990s, national government positions, shaped by direct representations from domestic fishing interests as well as governments' perceptions of the consequences of EU action (or inaction) on domestic fishing interests, were at the heart of the conflicts within the EU. Such conflicts, of course, led to more direct actions such as French fishermen blockading ports and fishing vessels of different nationalities accusing each other of cutting nets and other forms of sabotage (see Song 1995).

Despite the crucial importance of EU fisheries policy to the fortunes of both sides of the fishing industry in Europe and despite the organization of national fishing groups into one major European fisheries employers organization, there is little evidence that any of the major developments in EU fisheries policy can be attributed in any significant way to the activities of a European-wide group along the lines of a corporatist model. National fishing interests have to lobby both domestically and in Brussels. As Song (1995: 47) suggests, 'the fishing industries must make their case in Brussels as well, and government officials no longer prepare the management decisions of their governments. They prepare only the decisions of their governments on the points to be taken in Brussels.' In fact, Churchill (1987: 283) suggests that protests by fishing interests about 'lack of consultation' as well as the European Parliament's call for closer consultation in this area are symptoms of an inherently weak constellation of interests; 'while increased consultation is desirable, the Community must realise that as a group fishermen are less easy to consult with than many other occupations and groups because of fishermens' geographical and cultural isolation, their generally poor organization and the fact that fishermen (even from a single member state) do not share a view on every issue'.

This perspective on European-wide groups is one that is reflected more widely in the literature on European Union decision-making. McLaughlin and Jordan's (1993) study of the car industry shows that the multilateral character of policy-making in the EU can mean weakness for European groups, since individual firms can choose representation via the European group as *one* of its many possible strategies for seeking to influence EU decisions. It has the alternative of seeking direct influence for itself over the Commission or through national representation. As a consequence, 'the policy network has not assumed the cohesiveness or stability normally associated with a national "policy community". Furthermore it is also clear that where the Commission is sceptical of a group view, it will often test that position by seeking the opinions of individual group members' (McLaughlin and Jordan 1993: 145). This is consistent with Averyt's (1975) conclusion that closer relationships between national groups and national administration were associated with less effort devoted to lobbying the Commission. Moreover, McLaughlin and Jordan show the difficulty of maintaining anything resembling 'corporatist' arrangements in the policy-making system of the European Union. As in many other sectors, in the car industry the Commission appears to have been enthusiastic about the reform of industry representation into a single Association of European Automobile Constructors (ACEA), as opposed to the two organizations that preceded it. This resembles the sponsorship by government of interest organizations that is a frequently cited indicator of 'corporatist' patterns of group–government relationships. Despite some clear ACEA influence on EU policy, 'Consultation will often break down along nationalist and product lines, group cohesion is lost, and the dominant mode of contact can become bilateral' (McLaughlin and Jordan 1993: 157). Moreover, the Commission itself has some choice over which of the major producers it consults (McLaughlin and Jordan 1993: 152–3), one major characteristic of a weaker pluralist model.

Overall, the role of groups within policy-making, in so far as the European Commission is concerned, appears to be closer to the consultative pluralist model, where European-wide groups have limited powers to shape Commission policy directly, and where there is a potential for diversity among individual, sectoral, or national interest organizations, not only in the views that they represent but also in the strategies they choose to represent them. It must be emphasized that this says little about the power of groups within the EU *tout court*, but rather about the role in relation to the Commission's bureaucracy. It is quite possible that groups have a decisive influence on policy via national representations and the Council of Ministers. Conversely any weakness of groups within the Commission does not imply any unrestrained power of the Commission in relation to other EU institutions. Rather it suggests that the limitations that one might expect on the role of officials in the policy-making process provided by the fragmentation of authority in the European Union, and the multiple entry points that this offers to groups, are at least offset by the problems of internal cohesion among groups and the pursuit of diverse strategies of influence. Consequently, while not suggesting that officials 'dominate' in the EU policy-making process, there is little evidence to support the view that direct interest-group pressures weaken the status of Commission officials within the policy-making process, and of the four different views of group–government relations the available evidence suggests the current relationship approximates the one in Table 5.1 that gives the most prominent role to officials—the clientela or consultative pluralism cells.

3b. Subordinate legislation

Much EU legislation is equivalent to subordinate legislation in member states—statutory instruments and decrees and other laws made by bodies other than the legislature (Miers and Page 1982: ch. 6). In principle, all legislation by the major European institutions is *secondary* legislation in the sense that its authority derives from European Treaties. However, we may make a distinction between those regulations, directives, and decisions which require Council approval and those which do not. The latter we will term subordinate legislation (for a discussion of the difference between regulations, directives, and decisions see Lasok and Bridge 1982: ch. 4). Council approval may also require the submission of draft legislation to, depending on circumstances, one of the special committees (such as the Special Committee of Agriculture, the Committee of Permanent Representatives (COREPER), the Economic and Social Committee, the Committee of the Regions, and the European Parliament). Commission legislation can reach the *Official Journal* without reference to these other EU institutions. This distinction between Council and Commission legislation reflects the distinction between primary and subordinate legislation made in most member states (for a discussion in Britain see Miers and Page 1982). Table 5.3 shows that in numerical terms over 70 per cent of legislation is subordinate legislation.

As in national political systems, the fact that legislation is subordinate does not mean that it is less significant than other laws. Key issues affecting matters such as permissible national subsidies to ailing industries, the awarding of grants to major public works projects or the import levies and export refunds on certain goods are examples of issues covered by Commission legislation. Some areas, as one would expect, involve enormous amounts of subordinate legislation. Table 5.4

TABLE 5.3. *European legislation, 1980–1994*

Source of law	N	%
Commission Regulations	14,651	48.07
Commission Directives	380	1.25
Commission Decisions	6,577	21.58
Total Commission laws	21,608	70.90
Council Regulations	6,114	20.06
Council Directives	897	2.94
Council Decisions	1,859	6.10
Total Council laws	8,870	29.10
Total all laws	30,478	100.00

Source: CELEX EU Legislation CD-Rom (Context Electronic Publishers, London).

estimates the number of items of legislation for each directorate general.[2] Major producers of subordinate legislation include DG VI Agriculture (12,034 items), DG VIII Development (1,548), DG XIV Fisheries (1,464), DG XXI Customs and Indirect Taxation (1,248), DG V Employment, Industrial Relations, and Social Affairs (676), DG IV Competition (592), and DG III Industry (440). In *relative* rather than absolute terms those where there is least scope for subordinate legislation, i.e. where less than one half of the legislation passed relevant to that DG is subordinate legislation, include DG XXIII Enterprise Policy and Tourism; DG XIX Budgets, DG XII Science, Research, DG I External Relations, DG IX Personnel, DG XV Internal Market and Financial Services, DG II Economic and Financial Affairs, DG XVII Energy, DG VII Transport, and DG XVIII Credits and Investments. There is some correlation between the level of interest-group activity and the level of

[2] This estimate was derived by scanning the Justis CD-Rom for legislation with appropriate keywords; *author* keywords (Commission/Council), *form* keywords (decision, regulation, directive), selecting years through a *typdoc* (198* or 199*) keyword and *subject* keywords for each of the DGs. These were, respectively for DG I to DG XXI and DG XXIII: 'external relations or relations with', 'finance or economics', 'industry or industrial', 'competition', 'employment or industrial relations or social* not cohesion', 'agricultur* or veterin* or crop* or grain or meat or lamb or beef or pig* or corn* or maize or poultry or milk', 'transport', 'development', 'personnel'; 'audiovis* or cultur*'; 'environment* or nuclear safety or pollut*'; 'scien* or research'; 'communicat* or tele* or cultur*'; 'fish*'; 'market or financial institutions or direct taxation'; 'regional'; 'energy'; 'credit or investment'; 'budget'; 'financial control'; 'customs or indirect taxation'; 'enterprise* or tourism or distributive trad*'.

TABLE 5.4. *European legislation by Directorate General, 1980–1994**

	Commission laws	Council laws	% laws Commission	Court judgements
DG XXIII Enterprise Policy and Tourism	0	29	0	0
DG XIX Budgets	2	13	13	0
DG XII Science, Research*	54	236	19	0
DG I External Relations	353	1,463	19	8
DG IX Personnel	57	126	31	25
DG XV Internal Market and Financial Services	285	626	31	315
DG II Economic and Financial Affairs	2	4	33	0
DG XVII Energy	44	62	42	4
DG VII Transport	183	219	46	47
DG XVIII Credits and Investments	34	36	49	0
DG XI Environment, Civil Protection	287	265	52	104
DG XIV Fisheries	1,464	829	64	35
DG V Employment, Industrial Relations, and Social Affairs	676	359	65	78
DG XXI Customs and Indirect Taxation	1,248	647	66	31
DG III Industry	440	140	76	5
DG VI Agriculture	12,034	2,818	81	219
DG X Audiovisual, Communication	10	2	83	0
DG VIII Development	1,548	273	85	0
DG XVI Regional Policy	290	42	87	1
DG IV Competition	592	39	94	47
DG XIII Telecommunications	0	0		0
DG XX Financial Control	0	0		0
TOTAL	19,603	8,228	70	919

* Multiple entries for single laws possible.

Source: CELEX EU Legislation CD-Rom (Context Electronic Publishers, London).

regulatory activity (Tables 5.2 and 5.5); the number of interest groups mentioning contacts with a DG is higher where a DG is responsible for a larger number of secondary regulation ($r = +0.34$), but with only twenty-two cases this statistical relationship is not particularly strong.

The picture changes somewhat if one includes court cases initiated by the Commission over the same period. Here the largest number of court cases concern DG XV Internal Market and Financial Services (315) followed by DG VI Agriculture (219) and DG XI Environment, Civil Protection (104). While this does not refer to legislative activity, it nevertheless reflects the exercise of a degree of discretion by the Commission to seek to have applied through Court decision the provisions of European legislation as it believes they should be applied.

The significance of subordinate legislation for interest groups is twofold: first it allows interest groups to participate through the consultative bodies that have developed to advise the Commission as well as to scrutinize it in its legislative role; and second it offers greater potential scope for the development of more stable clientela relationships between groups and the Commission.

There are a number of committees which advise the Commission, primarily on the drafting of subordinate legislation but also on the drafting of proposals for Council legislation. Some of these committees are part of the system referred to under the term *comitologie*, according to which some committees have to be consulted before the Commission may use subordinate powers (see Ch. 6). There are also a large number of advisory committees outside the *comitologie* framework. The power of committees differs from committee to committee (see Docksey and Williams 1994; Buitendijk and van Schendelen 1995). The Commission publishes statistics on the meetings and composition of these committees. While we cannot assume that the Commission's figures give exhaustive coverage of the committees, and while one must also bear in mind that such committees are only an indicator of networks of consultation which also take place in *ad hoc* groups and informal meetings, they do suggest the areas of Commission activity that appear most open to group consultation.

The data in Table 5.5 set out figures on the number of members of such committees, the percentage of these members who are from private-sector organizations (i.e. those who are not national government or European Union officials), and the number of meetings of groups. In some DGs, most or all the consultative and advisory committees are governmental representatives (DGs I, IV, XXI, and VIII). These

TABLE 5.5. *Committees financed by the Commission budget, 1995*

	Total members	% outside government	N meetings
DG XII Science, Research	513	95.1	54
DG XXIII Enterprise Policy and Tourism	1.032	71.6	78
Secretariat General	961	68.2	101
DG V Employment, Social Affairs	7,706	67.5	812
DG X Audovisual Communication	177	61.0	18
Education Training Task Force/DGXXII*	2,650	59.4	198
DG XIII Telecommunications	2,053	58.2	170
DG XVI Regional Policy	467	45.6	51
DG XIV Fisheries	591	39.1	52
DG II Ec. and Fin. Affairs	1,487	38.6	75
DG XV Internal Market, Fin. Services	1,337	34.0	114
DG III Industry	3,912	32.6	472
DG IX Personnel and Admin.	83	32.5	24
DG XI Env., Nucl. Safety, and Civ. Protection	2,595	30.3	330
DG XIX Budgets	94	29.8	11
DG XVII Energy	843	28.9	64
DG VII Transport	1,348	24.5	157
DG VI Agriculture	14,359	21.3	1,065
DG VIII Development	414	12.8	40
DG IV Competition	620	10.2	71
DG I External Relations	1,070	6.5	110
DG XXI Customs and Ind. Taxation	2,233	3.4	194
TOTAL	46,546	37.5	4,262

* The Task Force on Human Resources, Education, Training, and Youth formed the basis of a new DG XXII in 1995.

Source: European Commission, *Statistiques réunions par DG pour l'année 1995*, BESTA 007 (Brussels, Commission of the European Communities, 1996).

contrast with others (DGs XII, XIII, the Secretariat General of the Commission, and DG V) where over two-thirds of members are drawn from outside government. However, if we look at the *absolute* numbers of non-official representatives DG V (5,201 private participants), DG VI (3,060), the Task Force on Human Resources, Education, Training, and Youth (1,574) and DG III (1,274) offer the greatest scope for group participation.

Is there any wider evidence of a clear pattern of group–Commission relations in the exercise of subordinate legislation? Here one would expect a stronger possibility of a much more stable form of relationship between the Commission and a few privileged groups—much closer to the clientela or corporatist pattern than the issue network-consultative pluralism that appears to dominate in policy initiation. Certainly there is little doubt that major groups, whether national or European in scope, develop close relationships with officials within the Commission. The value of such groups is that they can provide a stimulus for initiative, information, and expertise, and can broker compromises among potentially conflicting groups. Yet there is little evidence of whole sectors of policy being dominated by particular groups. In fact, we have relatively little evidence in so far as the mass of non-contentious Commission subordinate legislation is concerned. Given the fact that large numbers of national as well as European groups lobby the Commission directly, it is highly unlikely that any one or few of them can claim a monopoly on expertise. The evidence that exists on the Commission's use of its subordinate legislative powers over somewhat more controversial issues, however, shows little evidence of the decisive lobbying power of groups on their own.

This is shown quite clearly in the case of Thyssen Steel, which was widely acknowledged to have had a major role in the Commission's restructuring plan for the steel industry, but failed to prevent the Commission permitting major government subsidies to steel producers in Spain and Italy in 1994. The question of permitting steel subsidies, not least in the controversial Commission decisions (94/256/ESC to 94/261/ECSC) of spring 1994, was in fact settled after a change in the opinion of the Commission which had previously declared such subsidies unlawful. The reversal followed intense pressure from the Italian government and lobbying by Commissioners van Miert and Bangemann. The June 1994 decision to allow subsidies to Brescia, northern Italy, was the result of a vote in the Commission in which Sir Leon Brittan was the only opposing voice. This is similar to the story of the Air

France subsidy later in 1994. Jürgen Weber, chairman of Lufthansa, likewise looked to be in a strong position when, as a member of the committee set up to look at the future of the air industry, he helped write the report which envisaged state subsidies to airlines on a one-off basis to enable fundamental restructuring. Intense lobbying from both the French government and Air France allowed a £2.4 billion government subsidy, with a Commission vote which again Sir Leon Brittan, now with Henning Christophersen, opposed. Weber said of his role:

> The money for Air France is too high. It would cover our total group debt. . . . The EC did not consider our recommendations about ensuring this is the last time for Air France. . . . I don't know why I worked so hard for half a year on that committee when Brussels has thrown its report straight into the wastepaper basket (*Guardian*, 11 September 1994).

On some of the more controversial legislative acts of the Commission, three factors appear to have prominence. First the character of the commissioner: the change from Brittan, a British Conservative, to van Miert, a Belgian Socialist, in 1993 was widely predicted to mean a softer approach to state subsidies (Wolf 1993), just as Manuel Marín's assumption of the development aid portfolio led to an attempted shift from Africa to Latin America. Second, the relationship between the proposed act and the general state- or economy-building goals of European integration may be of great importance. Thus the Brescia subsidy was attractive because it offered the chance of keeping the steel rescue plans of the Commission on target, due to cuts in capacity promised as a result of the subsidy (*Guardian*, 20 May 1994). The Commission was prepared to face up to the most powerful cement-producers when it imposed substantial fines on those participating in a price-fixing cartel in November 1994. Third, lobbying appears to be at its most successful, as with initiating legislation that has to pass through the Council, when it has succeeded in enlisting the support of national governments through its ministers, permanent representatives, and the officials who represent it on the statutory and *ad hoc* committees within Brussels as well as commissioners.

4. CONCLUSIONS

It is not possible, of course, to characterize the whole of decision-making within the EU, at least as far as interest groups are concerned, as a system where interest groups are consistently powerful or consistently weak. Their power or role in policy-making must, as in member states, vary from issue to issue. However, such a characterization was not the purpose of this chapter. Rather, the objective was to examine whether there is any evidence to suggest that officials are particularly vulnerable to group pressures so that their autonomy and status in the decision-making process is limited by their dependence upon them. There is little such evidence. Most of the evidence points to a set of relationships somewhere between the clientela and the interest pluralism models. Certainly some groups may have developed a particularly close relationship with some DGs, or some directorates or sections of DGs. However, such relationships cannot resemble the corporatist or the issue-networks model, not least because the fragmentation of authority within the system, above all the powerful role of national governments within the EU, has a different impact on groups to that which results from the fragmentation of authority in the United States. In the European Union the available evidence suggests that fragmentation enables the lobbying of different institutions at different levels and serves to weaken the development of collective European strategies for exerting pressure on the Commission.

Within the Commission, we have little reason to believe that the relationship with interest groups weakens the role of the top EU civil service in policy-making. To be sure there are plenty of other factors weakening its role, not least the permeation throughout the whole EU system of the principle that national governments shape European policy. The evidence that EU officials listen to interests is certainly vast, yet there is also plenty of evidence that they are prepared to stand up against them by, say, taking them to court or passing legislation that directly harms their material interests. To stand up against such interests, whether it be over subsidies to ailing national steel industries or airlines, imposing fines on price-fixing cartels, or taking countries to court for the non-implementation of customs or environmental regulations, generates controversy. Such controversial decisions generally involve the political leaders of the Commission, the commissioners. The next chapter discusses the role of the commissioner in the EU bureaucracy.

6

Executive Political Control in the Bureaucracy

1. FORMS OF POLITICAL CONTROL

The notion of 'political control' over the EU bureaucracy is not directly equivalent to the notion as it applies in member states. Normally political control over the bureaucracy refers to the degree to which elected representatives, whether as parliamentarians, possibly also members of local and regional bodies, or whether as ministers, can constrain the actions of permanent officials. The relationship between parliament and the bureaucracy in the European Union can generally be discussed in terms of conventional models of legislative–executive relations of the sort found in nation-states. The European Parliament's role in the budgetary process and the passage of legislation is greater than that of many legislatures in member states (see Westlake 1994). The fact that Parliament poses a substantial constraint on the activities of the Commission as a legislator was discussed in Chapter 5. However, there is no direct equivalent to ministerial control in the European Union. The model of executive organization according to which a minister is a member of a government supported by a legislative majority (whether of a single party or a coalition) that obtains throughout Europe, even in semi-presidential systems such as France (Mezey 1995: 202), does not obtain in the European Union where there are two major sources of executive authority which may be expected to exert executive political leadership: the Commission and the Council.

The next part of this chapter explores the similarity and differences between commissioners and ministers as people who can exercise political control over the EU bureaucracy. The third part goes on to look at the skills and experience of commissioners and the fourth at mechanisms by which commissioners can seek to exert control within the Directorate(s) General for which they are responsible. The final part examines briefly the institutionalized political control that member states may exercise through their presence on statutory consultative committees —*comitologie*.

2. COMMISSIONERS—EUROPEAN UNION MINISTERS?

In the governmental systems of member states where legislative and executive branches are fused, political control can be relatively simply defined as the control by the minister—a politician selected from among the ranks of the governing party or parties to give political direction to a ministry. The legitimacy of a minister derives ultimately from the success of his or her party in legislative elections, even if not all ministers are themselves elected representatives (see Blondel 1985; Blondel and Thiebault 1991). Of course the dual executive system of France (to a much greater extent than found in other European countries with a directly elected President such as Ireland, Austria, and even Finland) makes this theoretical electoral chain of command less clear. Nevertheless, as an appointee of a prime minister the minister is responsible to a government that is in power because it has won enough seats to govern.

Ministers are exceptionally important figures in the democratic systems of European member states. They give leadership to public organizations on the basis of their *political* authority (see Page 1992). As the most important steering mechanisms, giving direction to government ministries, they are a crucial link between the electorate and public policy. As Rose (1987: 2) suggests:

> Any concept of government as a purposeful organization implies direction, and agents capable of carrying out the directives of policy-makers. . . . Popular elections place in office politicians who are the legitimate representatives of the will of the electorate. In a government without any steering capacity, elections would have little impact, for there would be no mechanism to give effect to the intentions of the governing party.

While there is little doubt that government can carry on functioning without effective ministers, under the political systems of Western Europe *democratic* government cannot.

In the European Union it is not possible to locate any such crucial instance of political control. The institution of the Commissioner comes closest to this ministerial model. The similarity between ministers and commissioners is that commissioners are for the most part (see below) politicians appointed by heads of national governments, usually after processes of intra- and inter-party bargaining, to lead major executive organizations for a limited period. The post is, however, a most curious one because it has little to do with being commissioned in any conventional sense of fulfilling a defined task on behalf of someone else. In European administrative history the commissary official played a fundamental role in state formation after the sixteenth century (Hintze 1964*a*). A *commissarius* was an official who was more directly answerable to the monarch than the *officier* who had come to occupy heritable or purchaseable posts removed from real royal authority. The *commissarius* was employed to do a specific set of tasks under direct control of the monarch and was hired and fired by him. The European commissioners are appointed by national governments who can fail to extend their appointee's period of office beyond four years, but national governments are unable to dismiss in mid-term and are expressly forbidden by the Treaty of Rome from seeking to influence Commissioners' decisions. There is provision in the Treaty of Rome (articles 157 and 160) for the Council or the Comission to apply to the European Court of Justice for a decision to dismiss an individual commissioner on the basis of misconduct or acting in breach of obligations. However, commissioners are independent of the Council of Ministers who cannot directly dismiss them. In fact, the only method of dismissing commissioners other than by a European Court of Justice decision is through censure by the European Parliament (see Clergerie 1995). Even here there is little resemblance between the traditional notion of a commissary and a European commissioner. Despite the fact that the 1995 Commission appeared before the European Parliament, the approval of which is required for a new Commission, there was no legal compulsion for it to appear (for a discussion of the process of parliamentary approval and its progress in 1995 see Maurer 1995). Moreover, only the Commission as a whole can be dismissed by Parliament not individual commissioners.

Although appointed by member states, with one coming from each of the smaller states and two each from Germany, France, the United Kingdom, Spain, and Italy they must, in their oath of office, swear that they 'shall not seek or accept instruction from any Government or any body'. This was the intention behind the Treaty of Rome, continuing the tradition of independence for the heads of the executive arm of the Community established beforehand in the High Authority of the European Coal and Steel Community (Schmitt 1962: 90 ff). Members of the

Commission are forbidden from any other employment during their period of office and are obliged to disclose their financial interests (although these, controversially, are not currently made public see Watson 1995). There are, of course, examples of occasions when commissioners are expected to act as officials who are affiliated to a member state. As one British commissioner, Sir Leon Brittan (quoted in Donnelly and Ritchie 1994: 35), suggested: 'I am frequently consulted by Jacques Delors (the President of the Commission) about what is going on in Britain. It would be bizarre if I could not answer. . . . I think that it is important that whoever holds my job should play an important part in British public life since the EC itself is part of British public life.'

Commissioners have been alleged to have used their positions on occasions to advocate national issues, such as when Sir Leon Brittan opposed the takeover of De Havilland by a Franco-Italian consortium (*Guardian*, 19 October 1991) or Jacques Delors was accused of sabotaging the GATT talks in 1992 (*Guardian*, 7 November 1992—for a discussion see Ross 1995: 176–80; Wealcode and Wallace 1995: 285–6). Possibly more striking evidence of an expectation that a commissioner does a national government's bidding occurred when, in February 1992, the Greek government announced that Vasso Papandreou would not be having her term renewed, the day after she had raised in print concerns (voiced elsewhere in the Commission) about the chances of Greece fulfilling the convergence criteria for monetary union. While the New Democracy government of Greece might not have been expected to reappoint a socialist appointee of the previous socialist government anyway, the timing of the Greek government's statement indicates an expectation that a Greek commissioner should not criticize its performance. It has become part of the lore of students of the European Union that commissioners do, in fact, represent national interests (Peterson 1995: 190).

The notion of a set of national interests is, of course, problematic since perceptions of national interests might differ within a single member state according to party or other standpoints, and they might differ from one national ministry to another, or one part of a national ministry to another. Even if we take a narrow definition of the term and understand it to refer to national interests as perceived by the permanent representatives of the member state, a characterization of commissioners as representative of nation-state interests is as implausible as the proposition that the perspectives and loyalties developed over, in many cases, a long political career are left behind as soon as a commissioner moves to Brussels. As Lord Cockfield (1994: 109) puts it

> As in all walks of life the degree of independence shown by individual Commissioners varies greatly. To be fair, one must start by accepting that we all bring with ourselves a baggage of preconceived ideas, outlooks and prejudices, many of them of a specific national nature. An Englishman does not think in the same way as a Frenchman, nor does a German share the same prejudices as an Italian. What at first sight appear to be a nationalistic motive may in fact be the honest expression of individual prejudices. . . . Nevertheless one must accept that . . . governments do exert pressure on their Commissioners.

He goes on to argue that the dividing line between lobbying and providing information is hard to draw—the United Kingdom permanent representative insisted on meeting him before each Commission meeting. He concludes 'I have no doubt that I was a great deal more independent than most Commissioners and while this did not endear me to some elements in London, it was an invaluable asset in dealing with other member states' (Cockfield 1994: 110).

The relationships between member-state government and commissioner are certainly variable and intricate. Yet this does not alter the fact that *commissioners are not commissioned by anyone to do anything in particular*. The question of executive political leadership within the European Union is complex. At one level it involves a study of the relationship between the Council as the body composed of the representatives of democratically elected governments and the other institutions of the EU. At another, political leadership by one member state can be exercised through skilful use of its permanent representatives and other representatives in negotiating in Brussels, also perhaps leaning on its commissioner(s) or any other sympathetic commissioner(s). These considerations, however, take us beyond the focus of this study, towards an understanding of the policy process within the EU and its member states and the circumstances under which the Council and member states can sustain their preferences in this policy process, as well as the circumstances under which commissioners can or might act independently of the wishes of their member states. Such questions are unlikely to be amenable to many useful generalizations, but a growing body of case-study material over the past decade has made us more aware of the fluidity of relationships of power within the European Union.

The purpose of this chapter is somewhat more limited than seeking general answers to the question of who governs in Europe. The central question addressed in this chapter approaches the issue of executive political control from the perspective of the EU bureaucracy. Commissioners manifestly do not have the direct political legitimacy that comes from moving into office following electoral success. Does this mean that they are less likely to be able to exercise control over the EU bureaucracy? Certainly the power of any one commissioner in relation to his or her permanent officials will depend upon factors such as the disposition of the commissioner and leading officials within the DG, the constellation of political forces surrounding a particular issue, as well as the relationship between the commissioner and colleagues in the College of Commissioners, including the President of the Commission. However, we can examine some of the evidence surrounding the environment in which commissioners can exercise control within their portion of the Commission. Such an environment is crucially shaped by two features of the Commission: the nature and skills of the people who become commissioners and the range of instruments at their disposal for imposing their stamp on the organization or organizations for which they are responsible.

3. SKILLS AND EXPERIENCE OF COMMISSIONERS

Members of the Commission are appointed by the governments of the member states for a five-year term—until 1995 the term was four years. Larger member states (France, Germany, Italy, Spain, United Kingdom) appoint two commissioners, the remainder one, giving a total of twenty members of the College of Commissioners. The governments of member states nominate candidates, and domestic political forces are certainly crucial in deciding who is nominated. Rumours often surround the precise reasons for a particular Brussels posting. The oft-cited grounds for nomination include rewarding loyal political support and providing a dignified exit from the domestic political scene, as well as supplying talented leaders for European public service. The Commission as a whole has to be approved by the European Parliament. Yet it is impossible to determine which factors weigh heaviest in most appointments.

The President of the College of Commissioners is agreed at the level of heads of government/head of state at the European Council, and the appointment lasts for two years.[1] The appointment of a successor to Jacques Delors in 1994 proved to be a particularly acrimonious process (Hooper 1994). Newspapers reported deals struck between countries whereby support for one particular candidate was rewarded with help over other issues, such as the location of one of the new agencies, or even with backing for favoured candidates for posts in the Organization for Economic Cooperation and Development, the Western European Union, or the World Trade Organization. Old scores were settled—Ruud Lubbers, the Dutch candidate, did not raise much enthusiasm from the German Chancellor, Helmut Kohl, because of Lubbers's critical stance as Dutch Prime Minister towards German unification in 1990. Lubbers's candidacy also attracted German opposition because the Dutch had opposed the location of the new Monetary Institute in Frankfurt (*Guardian* 1994). Britain's position on the succession question involved raising basic questions once again about the scale and pace of European integration (see Palmer 1994). Commissioners are certainly political figures in the sense that the process of nomination and appointment involves political controversy, potentially on a large number of dimensions.

Commissioners are also political figures since they generally acknowledge membership of a political party. Of eighty-six Commissioners for whom sufficiently detailed biographical information was available, seventy-eight (90.7 per cent) acknowledged membership of a political party, thirty-four (39.5 per cent) were members of a socialist or social democratic party, and forty-four (51.2 per cent) were members of a non-socialist party. There is a tendency to some balance in the partisan composition of the Commission representatives in the large countries which send two commissioners. The 1995 Commission contained two Spaniards, one a member of the socialist PSOE, the other a member of the People's Party; one of the German commissioners is a member of the Freidemokratische Partei Deutschlands, part of the coalition government with the Christliche Demokratische Union, while the other is a member of the socialist opposition, Sozialdemokratische Partei Deutschlands. The French commissioners are an ex-*Parti Socialiste* prime minister and a former ENA graduate who declares no party affiliation but has close associations with the centre right, since he was (then) Prime Minister Jacques Chirac's EC adviser in the late 1980s, he headed the French Interministerial Committee for co-ordinating

[1] There are currently two vice-presidents of the Commission selected within the College for a two-year term (up until the Maastricht Treaty of 1992 came into effect there were six—the Treaty allows for one or two vice-presidents).

TABLE 6.1. *Elective offices held by commissioners prior to Commission, 1967–1995*

Office	N	%
National legislatures	59	66.3
High party office	16	17.4
Local government	21	14.1
European Parliament	20	22.5
Regional assemblies	6	6.7
None	19	21.3
N commissioners	89	100.0

Sources: These include the following serial publications: *European Companion* (London, Dod's Publishing and Research); *Who's Who in the World* (Wilmette, Ill., Macmillan); *Who's Who in International Affairs* (London, Europa Publications), *Euro Who's Who* (Brussels, Éditions Delta); and *The International Who's Who* (London, Europa Publications).

European affairs under the centre-right Balladur administration in 1993, and served in Balladur's *cabinet*. One of the Italian commissioners likewise is not formally associated with any single political party while another was a Radical Party MP. Most countries tend to nominate an official associated with a governing party. Of the ten countries sending only one commissioner, only one, Erkii Liikanen from Finland, is associated with a party outside the governing parliamentary majority at the time of appointment.

Since commissioners are not publicly elected they cannot have the direct political mandate that comes from achieving office through electoral success. But they can have the political skills and experience that might be expected to accompany electoral success. Of the eighty-nine commissioners since 1967, seventy-one (78.7 per cent) have experience of elected office. Typically a commissioner will have held a seat in his or her national parliament: two-thirds of them did so. In addition they may have held a senior position within their political party (29.2 per cent). Just over one-fifth previously held seats in the European Parliament, although many of these will have been indirectly elected since they took up their seats before direct elections in 1979. Fewer commissioners declare that they have held regional office (6.7 per cent). Nearly one-quarter (23.6 per cent) have held local political office, but this

TABLE 6.2. *Previous ministerial experience of commissioners: highest post held*

	N	%
Ministerial office	50	56.2
Top posts	19	21.3
Junior government posts only	8	9.0
No ministerial office	31	34.8
TOTAL	89	100.0

Sources: *European Companion*; *Who's Who in the World*; *Who's Who in International Affairs*; *Euro Who's Who*; *The International Who's Who*.

figure is likely to underestimate local electoral experience since standard biographical references sometimes omit local political positions.

The fact that commissioners are usually, but not necessarily, chosen from the ranks of professional politicians reflects the general practice throughout the continent of Europe in the selection of ministers (Blondel 1985). Well over one-half of commissioners have occupied full ministerial posts in their national governments (Table 6.2). Some of the ministers who became commissioners (nineteen or 21.3 per cent) have occupied one or more of the most senior ministerial positions; three of these had been prime ministers (Gaston Thorn, Edith Cresson, and Jacques Santer), thirteen were former finance ministers, and seven had served as foreign secretaries. A large proportion, however, 34.8 per cent, had no previous ministerial experience, with a further 9 per cent having had experience only at a junior ministerial level.

The post of commissioner is largely a political one, filled predominantly by professional politicians, with four-fifths of commissioners having a political career before moving to Brussels. Over one-third have an occupational background in their home civil service (Table 6.3). Of these thirty-two, seventeen have been involved in diplomatic representation for part of their civil-service careers. Teaching and law are also important, followed by a range of other mainly professional occupations.

The wide range of experience that is brought to the post of the commissioner and the significant number of former civil servants who are appointed should not be taken to mean that, unlike many of their national ministerial counterparts, commissioners are specialists or even

TABLE 6.3. *Occupational backgrounds of commissioners*

	N	% of all commissioners*
Civil service	32	36.0
Diplomats	17	19.1
Education	24	27.0
Law	20	22.5
Private industry	13	14.6
Interest group	10	11.2
Journalism	10	11.2
Politics only	9	10.1
State industry	1	1.1
Other	3	3.4
TOTAL	89	100.0

Sources: *European Companion*; *Who's Who in the World*; *Who's Who in International Affairs*; *Euro Who's Who*; *The International Who's Who*.

particularly well qualified to fulfil the functions set out in their portfolios. While the question of the qualifications necessary for a senior politico-administrative position are open to debate, if we look at the 1995 Commission's portfolios and see whether there is anything in the previous experience of commissioners that makes them specialists in their areas (Table 6.4), we find that eleven of the twenty (Santer, Brittan, de Deus Pinheiro, De Silguy, Fischler, Flynn, Gradin, Liikanen, Monti, Oreja, van den Broeck) have past experience that has a close connection with their current responsibilities.

In terms of the type of incumbents it has attracted, the post of commissioner looks very much like a national ministerial post, apart from the very top rank positions. The incumbent is likely to be an MP, frequently with some other ministerial experience, although possibly somewhat more likely to have had ministerial or other experience in a field related to their portfolio as commissioner. One of the major differences between a post in the Commission and a post in a national government is that the countries tend to 'balance' the party-political affiliation of their commissioners, with the larger countries generally having one of their two commissioners chosen from the ranks of an opposition party.

The absence of a direct European electoral mandate marks commissioners off from their nearest counterparts, the ministers of member

TABLE 6.4. *Portfolios and previous experience of Commission members, 1995*

Commissioner	Responsibilities	Pre-Commission experience
Jacques Santer, President	Secretariat General, Legal Service, Security Office, Forward Studies Unit, Spokesman's Service, monetary matters, common foreign and security policy, institutional matters, and Intergovernmental Conference	*Close*: Prime Minister
Leon Brittan, Vice-President	External relations with North America, Australia, New Zealand, Japan, China, Korea, Hong Kong, Macao, and Taiwan; common commercial policy; relations with OECD and WTO	*Close*: Secretary of State for Trade and Industry
Manuel Marín, Vice-President	External relations with Southern Mediterranean countries, the Middle East, Latin America, and Asia (except Japan, China, South Korea, Hong Kong, Macao, and Taiwan) including development aid	*Remote*: Junior minister responsible for relations with the EC
Martin Bangemann	Industrial affairs and information and telecommunications technologies	*Remote*: Minister of Economic Affairs
Ritt Bjerregard	Environment and nuclear safety	*Remote*: Party leader, Minister for Social Affairs
Emma Bonino	Fisheries, consumer policy, and European Community Humanitarian Office	*Remote*: MP, MEP
Edith Cresson	Science, research, and development; Joint Research Centre; human resources, education, training, and youth	*Remote*: Prime Minister

TABLE 6.4. *(cont.)*

Commissioner	Responsibilities	Pre-Commission experience
João Rogado Salvador de Deus Pinheiro	External relations with African, Caribbean, and Pacific countries, and South Africa; the Lomé Convention	*Close*: Minister of Foreign Affairs
Yves-Thibault De Silguy	Economic and financial affairs; monetary matters; credit and investments; Statistical Office	*Close*: Many posts, including adviser with responsibility for European affairs and international economic and financial affairs, Prime Minister's Office
Franz Fischler	Agriculture and rural development	*Close*: Minister of Agriculture and Forestry
Padraig Flynn	Employment and social affairs and relations with the Economic and Social Committee	*Close*: Ministry for Industry and Commerce
Anita Gradin	Immigration, home affairs, and justice; relations with the Ombudsman; financial control, fraud prevention	*Close*: Junior Minister in Labour Ministry with responsibility for immigrant affairs
Neil Kinnock	Transport	*Remote*: Party leader
Erkki Antero Liikanen	Budget; personnel and administration; translation and in-house computer services	*Close*: Minister of Finance

Mario Monti	Internal market, financial services, and financial integration; customs; taxation	*Close*: Academic economist serving on many public bodies associated with competition and economic affairs and many company boards
Marcelino Oreja Aguirre	Relations with the European Parliament; relations with Member States; culture and audiovisual policy; Office for Official Publications; institutional matters and preparations for the 1996 Intergovernmental Conference	*Close*: Diplomat, Minister of Foreign Affairs
Christos Papoutsis	Energy and Euratom Supply Agency; Small business; Tourism	*Remote*: MEP
Hans van den Broek	External relations with the countries of Central and Eastern Europe, the former Soviet Union, Mongolia, Turkey, Cyprus, Malta, and other European countries; common foreign and security policy and human rights; external missions	*Close*: Minister of Foreign Affairs
Karel van Miert	Competition	*Remote*: Head of Private Office of Minister for Economic Affairs
Monika Wulf-Mathies	Regional policies; relations with the Committee of the Regions; Cohesion Fund	*Remote*: civil servant and trade union leader

states. Moreover, as Page and Wouters (1994) have suggested elsewhere, the fact that only 23 per cent of commissioners returned home to hold national electoral mandates has implications for the ambitions that commissioners bring to their executive leadership roles. Rose (1987: 74) discusses the 'engine of political ambition', according to which: 'From the perspective of an individual politician, what a ministry can do for his career is as important as what he can do for the ministry . . . Ministries work best when the skills and ambitions of ministers run parallel with the requirements of the ministries that they head.' Of course, there are notable exceptions to the tendency not to return to domestic electoral politics, including Raymond Barre (commissioner from 1967 to 1972) who went on to become Prime Minister of France (see also Page and Wouters, 1994a for further details). However, while a minister might have a relatively clear idea of the constituencies he or she addresses—the party, the faction, the electorate—and seeks to impress to improve a subsequent career, the job of commissioner makes it somewhat more difficult to identify such constituencies. There is no direct way of assessing the impact of the large-scale absence of domestic political ambitions on the quality of political leadership. We do not lack judgements about the qualities of different commissioners. Ross (1995: 160), commenting on the second Delors Commission, suggests that nearly half of them at least were unable or unwilling to have a major impact upon policy—three were 'out of their league', one was 'absent even when he was present', three were rather dull in clinging to the administrative side of their duties, and one was more concerned with running his business at home than with what went on in Brussels. We do lack any systematic evidence about whether this view would be supported by the experience of other Commissions, whether the EU is distinctive in this respect, and whether the same could be said about many national government cabinets. One can only suggest that it is possible that the EU commissioner career structure creates among incumbents of that office lower incentives to exercise distinctive political leadership.

Apart from the absence of an electoral mandate and the possible absence of the 'engine of ambition', commissioners appear to be otherwise as well qualified as, if not more qualified than, ministers in European member states to give direction to their organizations. Most have had active political careers including running for elective office and many have served in government in a senior position. Certainly some commissioners might have been poor politicians or become so—some seem uncomfortable and out of their depth in Europe. Others slip into the cut and thrust of Brussels life quite easily (see Ross 1995). Yet there is nothing inherent in the process of commissioner recruitment to suggest that commissioners are likely to be less able to shape what their officials do than their nearest counterparts in national capitals.

4. GIVING DIRECTION TO THE COMMISSION

The fragmented authority of the European Union places commissioners at a disadvantage, when compared with ministers, in their influence over the policy-making process. Aside from an electoral basis of authority, ministers in member states belong to a cabinet or council of ministers which in most countries, through the executive dominance of the legislative process, can virtually ensure that its decisions become law. The Commission can make no such assumptions about the fate of its decisions. As has been discussed above, the Commission cannot legislate outside its areas of subordinate legislation without the approval of other institutions, notably Council and the European Parliament. Even with subordinate legislation, the autonomy of the Commission is limited by the *comitologie* arrangement (see below). The fact that much policy-making is 'sectorized', with relatively little actually coming to the collective attention of a cabinet or council of ministers, gives the national government minister as chief sectoral executive substantial scope to make decisions without the direct intervention of the cabinet or any other bodies. In the European Union too, commissioners play a crucial role in such sectoral policy networks. Yet there are also institutions which serve to limit their scope for independent action to a greater degree than is common in member states.

The Commission is a collegial body. Individual commissioners do not have powers as such; rather, authority is vested in the Commission. A striking confirmation of this came when the European Parliament forced a commissioner to withdraw plans for a directive but the commissioner could not actually say he would withdraw it because he had not secured (collegial) Commission approval (Earnshaw and Judge 1993). Members are bound by collective decisions which can take the form of a majority vote when the preferred solution of a compromise or consensus cannot be achieved. While this is not so different from the cabinets or councils of ministers of member states, the range of responsibilities of commissioners are possibly more narrowly drawn than those of national ministers, involving greater likelihood that policy issues cut across the areas of responsibility of more than one commissioner. While such issues are more conventionally dealt with through direct contacts between the different commissioners or their representatives (in *cabinets* or officials from the relevant DGs), the College of Commissioners is important both as a forum in itself and as a basis for calculating whether to settle through bi- or multilateral compromise or to seek to raise an issue in the College.

The fragmentation of authority and the resulting limitations on the commissioner's capacity to take decisions without referring them to other loci of authority make the organizational and administrative resources that commissioners have at their disposal all the more important to the exercise of leadership within the Commission. The *cabinets* are potentially an exceptionally important aid to the commissioner in seeking to shape EU policy. *Cabinets* are frequently described as 'advisers' to the commissioner. Commissioners have an allocation of five *cabinet* members which will be paid for from EU funds (plus one extra, if a national from another country apart from that of the commissioner is appointed), and this is generally supplemented by officials seconded from the commissioner's home state. The average size of *cabinet* in the Santer Commission of 1995 was 7.75 members.

Membership of the *cabinet* is generally dominated by officials from the same member state as the commissioner. Ross (1995: 119) quotes an official from DG III who argued that 'cabinets are always pursuing their own national interests'. From our data set, almost all senior *cabinet* members were civil servants, either European or national civil servants. Of the sixteen c*hefs de cabinet* about whom information was available in our 1992–3 data set, thirteen had previously been civil servants. Of the seven deputy *chefs de cabinet* six had been civil servants. While ordinary *cabinet* members are not well covered in the biographical sources, of the eleven ordinary members, six had been civil servants, and six had been employed as school or university teachers. However, these figures are likely to be unreliable since the bibliographical sources are weakest on junior *cabinet* members, in part because those below *chef de cabinet* and deputy *chef de cabinet* are likely to be less prominent as bureaucratic or political figures and thus not yet included in major bibliographical sources.

While the trusted party colleague might be an important component of a *cabinet*, to have a serious chance of using the *cabinet* as an effective instrument for influencing policy-making in Brussels the balance is likely to be strongly in favour of those with some form of EU experience. When British commissioner Neil Kinnock appointed as his *chef de cabinet* Philip Lowe, a Director in DG IV who joined the Commission in 1973 and had already served in two *cabinets*, one as a director, this was taken to signal Kinnock's

> intention to become a heavyweight player in the European Commission power game by appointing an astute Eurocrat as the head of his political office. 'He could have chosen a reliable Labour supporter from his past who would have been outsmarted in the highly-specialised Brussels in-fighting. Instead he has picked a man who knows everything and everybody here. 'It's a clever move' a seasoned official said (Carvel 1994).

Those who have had experience dealing within the European Union, whether as European civil servants or those who, from the vantage point of a domestic ministry or from diplomatic service, are familiar with Brussels, are favourites for the leading positions within the *cabinets*. One official I spoke to described the normal *cabinet* balance as 'two-thirds insiders' to EU decision-making and 'one-third' outsiders. A permanent representative is normally included, as is a 'party hack'—a political friend from the member's home state. The available evidence suggests that 'insiders' are given prominence. Of the twelve *chefs de cabinet* in place in late 1995 about whom information was available, five were former EU officials, four were former diplomats, two were former permanent representatives of their country to the EU, and one was a civil servant with extensive diplomatic experience within his domestic Ministry of Economic Affairs. We must again bear in mind that the sparse coverage of *cabinet* members in the conventional biographical sources may bias the figures towards overestimating the number of senior officials within *cabinets*.

Cabinet members themselves are given portfolios—areas within the commissioner's range of functions for which they are responsible. Such portfolios change and the precise grouping of responsibilities can be the subject for negotiation between the commissioner and the President of the Commission (see Cockfield 1994: 30). *Cabinets* generally meet briefly on a daily basis (with or without the commissioner—this is likely to depend in part on the availability as well as the personal style of the commissioner). Advice is an important function of the *cabinet*, yet its members do far more than this. In a manner similar to the French model, they serve as the eyes, ears, and mouth of the commissioner within the Commission (Suleiman 1975). They alert their commissioners to issues, problems, and opportunities on the horizon. They may invoke their commissioner's authority in dealing with officials from their DG—a role that has to be handled especially delicately by those *cabinet* members who, as former EU civil servants, might be dealing with officials who were once and, at the end of their term in *cabinet*, might in future be their seniors. *Cabinets* conduct relationships between DGs and between commissioners, relations with the European Parliament, as well as relations between commissioners and those outside the EU—above all interest groups and political parties (for a discussion of the role of *cabinets* see also Docksey and Williams 1994).

The importance of the *cabinet* is highlighted by the fact that, unlike the position in countries such as America and Germany, there is little direct ability to change the composition of the top levels of the bureaucracy that a commissioner inherits. As has been shown above (see Ch. 4), the parachutists who reach top positions are not 'in-and-outers' who stay for a short time. In addition, officials with longer EU careers who are promoted to the top two ranks are also not likely to leave because of a change in commissioner alone. Thus it is quite possible for a Commissioner to have a Director General with whom he has very little in common. One extreme example of this was the case of Dieter Frisch, Commissioner Manuel Marín's Director General at DG VIII, who resigned in 1993 after joining the EU service in 1958. Although his resignation was ostensibly 'for health reasons', a letter to his friends and colleagues outlined a different story 'I am sad at heart. You know that it is not 'for health reasons' or 'on account of age'. The truth is that working relations with Vice-President Marín have deteriorated over the years to the point that I am no longer able to do a proper job' (Vallely 1993). The resignation of Director General Sigismundo Crespo in 1993, although a recent parachutee, following difficulties with his commissioner, Padraig Flynn, is another extreme example of commissioners thrown together with top officials with whom they cannot easily work (Leonard 1993). Both Flynn and Marín also used their *cabinets*, among other means, to bypass their top officials. Such public disagreements are, however, rare. Yet *cabinet* members can and frequently do establish direct contacts with officials in the Directorate General without involving the Director General.

Ross's (1995) discussion of the *cabinet* of Jacques Delors, the President of the Commission between 1985 and 1995, offers a remarkable picture of the potential importance of this institution. Delors gathered a team within his *cabinet* who shared his vision sufficiently to be able to work towards the goals which he identified, were skilled in recognizing problems and heading off potential opposition, and who established networks of support and loyalty throughout the EU. Together with his own gifts of leadership, he managed to play a decisive part in pushing the European Union out of its period of stagnation in the mid-1980s, a period known as 'Eurosclerosis', indicating a lack of vision and agreement about the future direction of European integration, towards the 1992 Single Market project as well as the commitment to further integration arising from the Maastricht Treaty of 1992. Ross (1995: 244) summarizes: 'The Commission was originally built to French administrative specifications, largely by Emile Noël, its long-term General Secretary. This French model, with which Delors and his able Commission team were intimately familiar, could thus be remoralized and mobilized quickly to generate the proposals needed to set the agendas that would optimize ideological and interstate conditions.'

5. INTERGOVERNMENTAL POLITICAL CONTROL

One of the important functions of officials in the Commission is to formulate subordinate legislation—the exercise of legislative powers delegated to the Commission. Such legislation, 'decree laws' or 'delegated legislation' in member states, is routinely passed without legislators being expressly asked to consent to the legislation, although in some countries, as in Britain with the Statutory Instruments Committee, committees of parliamentarians scrutinize the subordinate legislation and in principle may object to some items. Nevertheless, such *post hoc* powers of scrutiny by legislative committee are relatively weak powers of supervision over the bureaucracy when compared with the powers of supervision over the subordinate legislation of the Commission exercised by member states through the controversial committees systematized by the *comitologie* decision of the Council in 1987.

Under the 1987 decision there are a variety of different types of *comitologie* committees, chaired by a senior Commission official but generally composed of officials from member states (see Docksey and Williams 1994). Table 6.5 tabulates the 249 committees for which the Commission budgeted in 1995 (a further thirty-two had entries in the budget but no budget item). The most common of these are the advisory committees, of which there are 125. The advisory committees have the right to be consulted but the Commission only has to take the

TABLE 6.5. *Statutory Committees of Compulsory Consultation, 1995*

	Type of Committee					
	I	II(a)	II(b)	III(a)	III(b)	TOTAL
Consumer policy	0	0	1	1	1	3
Enterprise, Tourism	0	0	2	0	0	2
Development	1	0	1	2	0	4
Environment, Nuclear Safety	3	4	0	4	10	21
Statistical Office	2	1	5	1	0	9
Customs and Direct Taxation	16	2	0	15	2	35
Industry	10	0	0	8	0	18
Transport	9	1	0	7	0	17
Energy	4	1	0	1	1	7
Employment, Industrial Relations, and Social Affairs	14	0	1	3	0	18
Agriculture	3	30	1	8	0	42
Internal Market and Financial Services	14	1	1	2	1	19
Education, Training, Youth	4	0	1	0	0	5
External Relations	28	0	0	1	0	29
Economic and Financial Affairs	2	0	0	0	0	2
Competition	5	0	0	0	0	5
Audiovisual, Information, etc.	1	0	0	0	0	1
Science, research	1	0	0	0	0	1
Telecommunications	6	0	0	0	0	6
Fisheries	0	3	0	0	0	3
Regional Policies	1	0	0	0	0	1
Budgets	1	0	0	0	0	1
TOTAL	125	43	13	53	15	249

Note:
I: advisory Committee; II: Management Committee (II(a) no enforced deferral; II(b) with enforced deferral); III: Regulatory Committee (III(a) with 'net' procedure; III(b) with 'safety-net' procedure).

Source: *Official Journal of the European Communities*, L369, 37 (31 Dec. 1994), 504–16.

'utmost account' of the opinion. The management committees (of which there are sixty-six) have more extensive formal powers since they may refer a measure to the Council. Under type II(a) the management committee does not have to defer implementation of the measure, under type II(b) it has this power. The regulatory committees require a qualified majority for the measure to be enacted, without it the measure is referred back to the Council which itself has to be accepted or rejected by a qualified majority (type III(a), the 'net' procedure) or simple majority (type III(b), 'safety net' procedure).

As Buitendijk and van Schendelen (1995) state, the role and importance of committees in the European Union cannot be determined by their formal status alone. Each type of *comitologie* committee establishes the principle of direct member-state involvement in the subordinate legislative powers of the Commission. The genesis of the *comitologie* system in 1987 offers evidence of the intention of the Council to use such committees as means of Council scrutiny and control of the subordinate legislative process, since it based it on article 145 of the Treaty of Rome, which supported a more extensive role for the Council, than the other possible legal basis, article 155, which implied greater discretion for the Commission (see Blumann 1989). As Docksey and Williams (1994) suggest, this means effectively that proposals generally have to be cleared with member-state officials as they are being drafted and before they are formally sent to the committees. This is a form of political supervision of the bureaucracy not generally found in nation-state systems, which generally leave the responsibility of identifying and objecting to subordinate legislation to the legislature. In the European Union, while the formal powers of the committees vary, they give member-state officials the chance to participate in shaping the whole range of Commission legislation.

6. CONCLUSIONS

In the European Union context the notion of political control differs from that of the administrative systems of member states, since there are two broad political instances which might exercise control: member-state governments and commissioners. In this context political neutrality, a notion associated with many but not all European civil services, is an elusive concept. Commission officials are expected to support the aims of strengthening European integration. This expectation was given resounding expression after the publication of a book in autumn 1995, critical of the Exchange Rate Mechanism and the creation of a single currency, by Bernard Connolly, a head of unit in DG II, who was consequently dismissed (*The European*, 7–13 Sept. 1995). While appointments and promotions are certainly made involving criteria that can be called 'political' (see Ch. 3), there is little direct evidence of *party*-political appointments, and no major cases raising such appointments taken to the European Court (apart from Judgement of the Court of First Instance, 8 Nov. 1990, Brigitte Bataille *v.* European Parliament (case T–56/89), concerning the demarcation between party group officials and Parliament Secretariat officials).

What are the implications of the EU pattern of institutionalizing political control? One possible consequence is the creation of tensions within the EU civil service between those officials who owe their position to the politicians who appointed them and those career officials who have worked their way up to senior positions. At the top of the EU civil service such relationships are complicated by the fact that there are, in this context, three broad types of officials; those most closely associated with the commissioner within the *cabinets*; those who have reached senior positions (including A1, A2, and to a lesser degree A3) through nomination or support from their home states in the EU bureaucracy; and senior officials (including some A3 and most below this) who may be classed as career officials. Certainly, there are some combinations of these three types, including many career EU officials who are appointed to the normally 'political' top three ranks. As has already been discussed (see Ch. 4), there is evidence from surveys as well as the comments of many EU officials of a widespread perception of a distinction between political and career officials, as well as a degree of resentment that the top ranks of the EU bureaucracy are closed to career officials without political contacts. Two officials expressed this with much vitriol when they complained of 'the contradictions of a would-be management riddled with politically appointed puppets, with more than a few outright incompetent rejects from national Civil services to top it all up and maintain administrative coverage' (Beuzard and White 1992). That the *cabinet* system significantly adds to this perception of differences at the top cannot be doubted—there have been at least two well publicized cases over the past few years of top officials falling out with members of the *cabinet* (see p. 128 above). Moreover, relationships between *cabinet* members and Directors, Deputy Directors General, and Directors General have to be handled delicately to avoid such breakdowns.

However, it is important not to exaggerate the potential for a three-way conflict between, broadly, A1–A3 officials, *cabinet* members, and the rest. First, A1–A3 officials might themselves develop very close working relationships with *cabinets*. Lord Cockfield (1994: 42) points out that the Completion of the Internal Market programme relied heavily on the co-operation with him and his *cabinet* of Directors General and Deputy Directors General, some of them outside DG III, and he stressed the importance of the Deputy Director General in DG III:

> Paolo Cecchini who subsequently achieved fame as the author of the Cecchini Report which was to analyse in the most convincing way the benefits of the Internal Market Programme. He was a personal friend of Adrian Fortescue, my Chef de Cabinet, and he did more than anyone to prepare me for the forthcoming negotiations on the allocation of the Commission portfolio.

While conflict is one possible result of the relationship between *cabinet* and permanent officials, co-operation is another, and indifference yet a third. There are possibilities for the *cabinet* effectively to bypass an official of senior rank, and there are opportunities for that official to devote attention to concerns that do not impinge on the priorities of the commissioner and his or her *cabinet.* Much depends upon the personalities involved and their respective interests, skills, and status within the Commission.

As was noted in Chapter 1, extensive politicization of administrative appointments has the potential to reduce the overall status of a civil service as career progress within it relies upon political contacts rather than competence or technical ability. However, as has already been mentioned in Chapter 4, the main problem here is with the nation-state role in appointing senior officials, which not only causes resentment among career officials in the EU but has also been responsible for some spectacularly inappropriate appointments. However, such obvious mismatches are rare. Moreover, nearly two-thirds of top officials appointed in this way have proved themselves in their own national civil services. This means that the impact of the power of national patronage on the overall technical competence and status of the EU civil service is limited.

7

Conclusions

1. INTRODUCTION

So what, then, is the character of the EU bureaucracy? Is it an entirely new form of administration, with little more than superficial features in common with existing forms of bureaucracy, whether national or international? Moreover, and this was the central point of looking at the character of the EU as a bureaucracy in the first place, what systematic impact does it have on the policy process of the European Union? The purpose of this chapter is to give some direct answers to these questions. Section 2 reviews the major conclusions of the chapters. The following section begins to take us beyond these findings to look at the wider consequences of the character of the EU bureaucracy on patterns of policy-making in the EU in the light of David Coombes's (1970) influential characterization of the role of the EU bureaucracy in policy-making. Section 4 discusses some of the problems of this analysis and uses a more discriminating framework to review the work of the Commission's civil service and its role in the policy-making process. Here it must be admitted that the evidence on which to base an assessment of the role of the civil service is limited. There is, of course, a large and growing number of studies that examine policy-making in the EU. However, there is a quite legitimate tendency in very many of them to regard the Commission or at least the DG as the relevant actor—'the Commission revised its proposals' or 'DG XIV has tended to develop a closer interest in . . .'. Relatively rare are the glimpses of the intra-mural politics of the DG or directorate. Nevertheless it is important to examine civil-service activity in the light of what is known about its role. The final section discusses the nature of political control over the civil service within the EU and sets out the fundamental difference between political supervision as understood in European nation states and the European Union.

2. CHARACTER OF THE EU BUREAUCRACY

If one looks at *cohesion*, in many respects the EU civil service is no less cohesive in terms of its formal structures and career patterns than many member-state administrative systems. There is a service-wide pattern of recruitment and promotion, and a significant degree of mobility within it. This is not to suggest that there are no 'turf' conflicts over responsibility for a particular issue among Directorates General or within them. Competition and Industry, for example, have notoriously had different views about the desirability of mergers and state subsidies (Wilks and McGowan 1995). There are, in environmental policy, distinctive and sometimes conflicting approaches adopted by 'business friendly' DGs and those favouring stricter EU pollution regulation (Berger and Skærseth 1994). The short lived DG XXII responsible for Cohesion was the subject of major divisions, not least between DG IV (Competition) and DG XVI (Regional Policy) (Wishlade 1993; Hooghe 1994). The whole area of consumer policy is divided among different DGs, and the Consumer Policy Service's weakness is compounded by the 'lack of active cooperation between different consumer services' (Gozens 1992: 78). But such conflicts are an inevitable feature of any organization. The division of labour produces organizational structures which not only give individuals power within them and in general a desire to maintain if not expand that power, but also engender different perspectives on appropriate policy responses (Allison 1971).

There are many things on which EU officials see each other as clearly on the same side, such as pay and conditions of work. A survey suggests that Commission officials are significantly less likely to believe that 'personal rivalries' are a major feature of working life than employees in private industry and other public services, and 'team spirit' is somewhat higher than among employees outside (European Commission 1988). Among EU officials there is also a very clear sense of mission—an identification with the Commission's goals of working towards an ever closer union. As two anthropologists argue

> If the public at large remain unaware of their European identity, the same cannot be said of the Commission bureaucrats. Indeed, something of an embryonic European culture does appear to be emerging within the Community institutions, as for all that the different institutions may often disagree over goals, their staff share a similar set of experiences and lifestyles, certain distinctive patterns of behaviour, and a common (bureaucratic) language. Whether this

> will provide the engine needed for a new type of pan-European identity and consciousness—just as intellectuals and romantics in the last century were the pioneers of nationalist consciousness—or whether instead it will remain the culture of an isolated international bureaucratic elite—remains to be seen (Shore and Black 1992: 11).

This is supported by the survey, cited above, which suggests that 70 per cent of officials believe it is important to have a 'sense of commitment to the European ideal' (European Commission 1988).

The most distinctive characteristic of the EU administration is its multinational character. The fact that its members come from different parts of the EU, with different administrative and political cultures (see Hofstede 1980), has been taken by many to mean some sort of basic lack of cohesion: an incompatibility between people operating with different national 'styles' (Abeles *et al.* 1993). There are undoubtedly different ways of going about things in different nations. Moreover, officials will generally try to deal, at least in the first instance, with people from the same country or from the general geographical area ('north' or 'south'). However, the evidence to suggest that such distinctions produce separate patterns of thought and communication and that this creates an administration fragmented along national lines is very weak (see Egeberg 1995). Just as any organization, whether local, national, or international, is made up of people of different outlooks or ways of dealing with other people, the fact that some such differences may (correctly or incorrectly) be explained through use of national stereotypes hardly constitutes fragmentation. The EU seems to have successfully prevented the permanent positions in the higher reaches of any particular, discrete service from being the preserve of any one nationality. Any dominance of single nations in the policy process is more possible in the College of Commissioners itself than the civil service, since the *cabinets* are dominated by members from the commissioner's home state.

A more significant impact of nationality in the permanent EU civil service is that the quest for national balance has created a process feared by many EU officials: the 'renationalization' of the bureaucracy. Not only are the senior ranks of the EU service the main preserve of those (whether EU officials of outsiders) who have been put forward or whose appointment has been agreed by representatives of member states, at a less senior level a very large numbers of officials are not themselves EU employees, but officials on contract or secondment (Dubois

1993: 82–3). This renationalization has not only as its consequence a perception among EU officials that the service itself does not reward merit. There is also some evidence that it contributes towards a sense of isolation among officials at the senior levels. One career Commission official explained to me that in the surrounding offices were people whose precise status in the EU was unclear; of parachuted officials there was often the suspicion that they had been sent by their home civil services to achieve something or to prevent something; seconded officials spending a short time in the EU might be there for the same sort of reason; both seconded and contracted officials might be looking for a more permanent EU position, with the possibility that they would pursue this by, say, helping a Commissioner of their nationality or currying favour with an official from another DG. Permanent career officials themselves overwhelmingly believe that political contacts are the most important means of progressing within the EU (European Commission 1988). Given the fact that colleagues can be assumed to be following rather diverse career paths within the EU, and it is never clear precisely who is following which, the question of loyalty and trust is rather problematic; above a certain level it is clear that one's reputation or achievements within the DG or the Directorate are not the most important factor shaping one's career. The official raised the question of why one should, say, share the results of one's own hard work when asked for information, when there is the possibility that this will be used to promote another's career or even possibly be used against one.

This problem of trust, somewhat reminiscent of Michel Crozier's (1964) diagnosis of the cultural pattern of French bureaucracy in his *Bureaucratic Phenomenon*, was observed also by Coombes, who alluded to Crozier's work:

> Delegation becomes increasingly difficult in practice because of the lack of confidence in subordinates who might be members of other 'parties'. . . . The vicious circle of bureaucracy now sets in. Many of these tendencies were reported to us by officials of the Commission, and we found some evidence of them in our study of personnel administration (Coombes 1970: 259).

The Commission's survey also showed that, 'on the whole, contact with other Commission staff—except for close working colleagues . . . — was felt to be poor' (European Commission 1988: 4). One must not exaggerate the strength of the evidence on this, however the diverse career paths which result from the multinational character of the bureaucracy do, appear to contribute towards a degree of fragmentation, even within a Directorate, based on uncertainty over motives and loyalties.

There is no distinctive caste among top EU officials which corresponds to the way that Oxbridge officials dominated, and to a lesser degree still dominate, the upper reaches of the British civil service or that law graduates fill the majority of senior posts in the German civil service. Law and social-science degrees are the most common qualifications held by top officials. Clear evidence of national traditions is observable in the educational qualifications of officials; British and Irish officials being disproportionately arts educated, while Germans have proportionately the most lawyers. However, overall, the social sciences are among the most popular degrees for officials in the EU. The higher reaches of the EU administration are dominated by males with middle-class origins, but this is nothing unusual in national bureaucracies (see Aberbach, Putnam, and Rockman 1981).

There is certainly plenty of evidence that interest groups have helped shape many major areas of EU policy. Moreover, the influence may be stronger in some parts of the EU bureaucracy than others—Padgett (1992) argues that the Competition Directorate General is handicapped by a shortage of specialists in energy and as a consequence was especially vulnerable to group influence. Nevertheless, the evidence is weak that this influence is channelled through a permeable bureaucracy, a bureaucracy which is generally vulnerable to group pressures in the same way that 'issue networks' constrained the power of executive organizations in the United States in the 1970s (Heclo 1978; Jordan 1981). The distinctive role of interest groups in the European Union lies in the multiple access points that exist to shape policy—not only through direct links with Commission officials, but also through domestic governments, permanent representatives, established and *ad hoc* consultative arrangements, as well as the European Parliament. Given the diversity of groups and points of access there is little evidence of the Commission bureaucracy being systematically limited in its power to initiate or enforce legislation because of the power of a particular group or set of groups.

The powerful role of representatives from member states in the appointment of top officials at first appears equivalent to the practice of making political appointments in countries such as the United States. As a form of political control of the bureaucracy this is exceptionally limited. Political appointees remain in the bureaucracy for a long time, and this is likely to continue well after the reason (assuming there was one) for placing them in the position has been forgotten. As anxieties about 'renationalization' suggest, EU civil servants fear an intrusion of national political interests into the administrative fabric of the Commission, through the hiring of national experts on temporary contracts or similar arrangements. This is likely to be a more direct and responsive route for national influence than, say, an economics professor who happened to find favour with the government before last of a particular member state. The *cabinet* structure does, however, provide the commissioner with a potentially powerful means of keeping track of what goes on in his area of responsibility and asserting his authority throughout it. Ross's (1995) pathbreaking account of the Delors experience shows how *cabinets* are crucial tools in mobilizing support within and outside the Commission for any significant political project.

Despite the aspirations of Jean Monnet to create a new form of organization, the EU bureaucracy was essentially constructed as a traditional bureaucracy, such as one might find in many continental member states. It is hierarchically structured in the sense that authority comes from the political apex and flows down, with recruitment and career structures based on expertise, length of service, and points systems which were the dominant pattern in Europe in the decades after the Second World War (see Chapman 1959). Yet the EU does not have the constitution of a traditional European state. While merit, technical qualification, and length of service apply fully below the very top administrative ranks, nationality is crucial in at least the top three levels. Even lower down in the bureaucracy the traditional pattern of civil-service career structures is qualified by a whole range of exceptions, such as the appointment of non-establishment officials on secondment or contract. The fact that it is a multinational bureaucracy has a fundamental impact upon its cohesion, demographic character, permeability, and the form of political control, since the EU civil service is part of two different worlds similar to what Damaška (1986), analysing the process of justice, terms contrasting 'ideals of officialdom' (Damaška 1986: 17).

> The first structure essentially corresponds to conceptions of classical bureaucracy. It is characterized by a professional corps of officials, organized into a hierarchy which makes decisions according to technical standards. The other structure has no readily recognizable analogue in established theory. It is defined by a body of nonprofessional decision makers, organized into a single level of authority which makes decisions by applying undifferentiated community

standards. The first structure I shall call the *hierarchical* ideal or vision of officialdom, and the second I shall call the *coordinate* ideal.

These structures and the ideals which result from them are structures of *authority*; one in which 'officials are locked into a strict network of super- and subordination' and another where 'they are rough equals, organized into a single echelon of authority'.

In the context of the EU we find strong elements of both ideals of officialdom actually coexisting. The two ideals of authority reflect two different arenas in which officials must operate, rather than philosophies underlying the structure of distinct organizations. As officials appointed and promoted (at least below the A3 level and to some extent above) on merit and length-of-service criteria, they belong to a hierarchically structured organization which applies norms and offers advice on the basis of technical expertise, and operate in a *bureaucratic arena*. On the other hand, EU civil servants belong to an organization whose multinational character can shape internal organization, careers, and relations with outside groups and with political masters. Its direct political master, the Commisson, does not have control over the legislative process. As a consequence, we know that officials are involved in seeking to mobilize support among other EU institutions and member states; they operate in what we might term an *intergovernmental-interinstitutional arena*, since it requires the mobilization of political support among member states as well as other EU institutions, possibly also other international organizations (such as the United Nations or NATO) rather than predominantly technical expertise. Discussions of European integration have long debated the relative importance of nation states, economic pressures, and functional 'spillovers' in explaining the pace and character of European integration (George 1991: ch. 14). To give prominence to the term 'intergovernmental' indicates the centrality of member-state support for EU legislation. Despite the growing importance of other European institutions (such as Parliament and the European Court of Justice) intergovernmental agreement through the Council remains the most important constraint on EU action, and the most important buttress for the influence of interest groups within the EU. Of course, the coupling with the term 'interinstitutional' suggests it is not the only constraint.

Does this mark the EU out from other European member states? There are differences between countries in terms of the degree to which the legislature is dominated by the executive (Mezey 1995), yet the relative weakness of the Commission when compared with the executive of member states is of an entirely different order. A large proportion of Commission proposals find their way into EU legislation (Ch. 5). However, proposals are rarely formally put forward until they have been negotiated with those whose agreement is essential—above all, member states, sufficient support from which in the Council is a *sine qua non* of major policy change. This twofold characteristic of the EU bureaucracy as a traditional bureaucratic organization in an essentially non-bureaucratic setting, where the Commission has to engage in the mobilization of support throughout other institutions as well as member states, lies at the heart of many discussions of the influence of the bureaucracy on the pattern of policy-making in the EU, and one of the earliest as well as the most systematic expositions of this dual role is found in the work of David Coombes.

3. THE IMPACT ON POLICY-MAKING: THE COOMBES THESIS

One of the most consistently observed impacts of the character of the EU bureaucracy on EU decision-making is broadly along the lines that the traditional bureaucratic character of the EU administration subverts or at least weakens the political impetus towards closer EU integration. This was the central point made twenty-five years ago by David Coombes (1970) who explored the dual role of the European bureaucracy. The Commission, as the largest component of this bureaucracy, Coombes argued, had both a bureaucratic and a political leadership role. The Commission is, in his terms, a 'bureaucracy', since it has tasks 'normally associated with the administrative function in a national political system'. However, at the same time its founding fathers expected it 'to impel other parts of the Community by the exercise of various forms of political leadership' (Coombes 1970: 118–19). This function of political leadership was to be filled by the 'Initiative function (inventing and "selling" means of extending the scope and level of integration) together with the Normative function (legitimizing with its uniquely European character and defining the common interest)' (Coombes 1970: 296–7). The main thrust of his analysis was to show that the promise of the early days, or at least the hopes of the founding fathers of the European Union, were short lived. 'The Commission of President Hallstein (and, we have reason to believe, the High Authority of Jean

Monnet) at least in the first three years of its existence was not a bureaucracy' (Coombes 1970: 299). Yet as the administrative tasks have developed, the Commission has become swamped by its administrative function and has taken on the 'conservative, mechanistic and impartial' character of traditional bureaucracies and 'cannot be called on to take initiatives or to hold convictions' (Coombes 1970: 298).

It might be objected that Coombes's description of the 'bureaucratic' process of European Economic Community decision-making certainly has little direct resonance in the European Union of today because of enlargement and massive economic, social, and political change in Europe between 1970 and 1995. However, it is surprising how well his broad conclusions hold up to the test of twenty-five eventful years. Ludlow (1991: 85–6) argues that the Commission is 'in many important respects very much the institution that it has always been . . . Its basic organizational units are much as they were in 1967. . . . Even its structural weaknesses, so clearly analyzed in 1979 in the Spierenberg Report, are for the most part still there'. Featherstone (1994: 165) also endorses Coombes's diagnosis of a lack of political leadership towards closer integration.

Even the fact that European integration has certainly progressed further than Coombes appeared to be suggesting was possible at that time does not require much of a revision of the Coombes thesis. The Delors period (1985–95), above all, seems to indicate that the Commission is capable of exercising the sort of leadership that to Coombes appeared to be ruled out by its routine bureaucratic characteristics. Nevertheless, the broad outlines of the 'Delors method', as set out by Ross (1995) or Grant (1994), are similar to Coombes' characterization of the innovative period under Walter Hallstein (1958–67). The Hallstein presidency is

> best typified by making an analogy with a political party or highly organized pressure group rather than with an administrative organization. This organization was held together largely by common loyalty and understanding—there was little demand for mechanical rules and regulations and little stress on hierarchical lines of command. The values esteemed in this organization were energy, enthusiasm and creativeness. . . . [Generally reluctant member states] were led to accept European measures through the short-term, selfish advantages they could get from them. This procedure often involved, as we have seen, tortuous bargaining on matters of incredible detail. The main strategy of the Commission was to work through national officials and interest groups and to get the national governments into a position where they had to agree to a Community solution or else have nothing at all (Coombes 1970: 311).

This would also be recognizable as a brief appraisal of the Delors approach as well, although to Delors's great skills of statesmanship should be added an ability to manœuvre himself into a dominant position *within* the EU politico-administrative organization. Delors's transformation of EU politics is all the more remarkable since he did not have the favourable political climate for European integration that made Coombes believe the Hallstein period was unique. Yet, Coombes was not suggesting that such initiatives by outstanding entrepreneurs were impossible within the EU: he argued that, under some circumstances at some times, it was possible for the 'political leadership' role of the Commission to re-emerge and predominate (Coombes 1970: 299).

As a characterization of the impact of the EU bureaucracy on EU policy-making there are two major shortcomings with the Coombes thesis. First, the conception of political leadership as the political impetus to closer integration might have been appropriate in the earlier years of the EU when the functional concerns of EU policy were more limited. It cannot be denied the forging of an ever closer union is now an important factor giving continuity to a wide range of EU policies. However, to view the tensions in the European civil service as almost exclusively tensions between a European-integrationist impulse and the deadweight of bureaucratic inertia and national resistance has become increasingly less relevant to the character of policy-making in the European Union. It has been overtaken by the expansion of the EU not merely in membership but in its range of responsibilities.

The powers of the European Union have grown dramatically. In Chapter 2 it was established that the staff of the EU is now nearly six times the size it was in the late 1960s (see Fig. 2.1), its budget grew from 0.48 per cent of the GDP of EU member states in 1969 to 1.2 per cent in 1995 (European Commission 1995: 34–5), and the volume of regulations passed rose from 1,908 regulations, 252 directives, 1,769 decisions in 1969, to 37,822, 2,750, and 14,063 at the end of 1994. There are, of course, many new areas for EU regulation to pioneer closer European integration. However, there are very many areas which have already been the subject of regulation, and the question of using, elaborating, or reshaping existing regulation is at least as important as opening up new areas for European co-operation. The political leadership in the new European Union is somewhat different to that of the old. While the drive towards closer integration is certainly one form of leadership that one might look for within the European Union, the expansion of the functions of the organization calls for another—one that gives guidance to the organization which bears some relationship to external preferences (see Ch. 6). As Max Weber (1988: 393–4) argues:

> The meaning of active mass democratization is this: political leaders are no longer chosen by virtue of their esteem among a small group of dignitaries . . . but through winning the trust and faith of the masses, and thus coming to power through means of mass demagoguery. This means, in fact, a caesaristic form of leadership selection. And in fact every democracy leans towards this.

Given that European integration remains an important goal, and given that very large areas of public policy are decided within the European Union, we might expect to find political leadership in areas such as regulation and subsidy of agriculture, trade, social policy, and regional development, for example. This might be termed a more routine form of political leadership: it might not produce constitutional leaps forward but rather offers the chance for politicians to guide policy in an intended direction. The problem with the Coombes thesis is that it does not say very much about these wider aspects of political leadership.

To some extent this is not a particularly damaging criticism of the Coombes thesis. It is possible to adapt his basic argument to a variety of different contexts, not just leadership conceived as closer integration. If one takes this secular view of the nature of political leadership as routine leadership, there is still a remarkably high degree of agreement among authors on the basic problem of coming up with many major innovations—producing initiatives which provoke controversy and which could not have been expected from the routine consensus-mongering of bureaucratic politics. The problem is the absence of a single source of authority, usually associated with the cabinet form of government which is the dominant model within European nation states. Commissioners can be and have been quite publicly outvoted in how they handle their own portfolios (Berger and Skærseth 1994); votes in the Commission are on many controversial issues well known. The process of decision-making in the EU allows the direct participation of member-state representatives, whether through COREPER, *comitologie*, or on an *ad hoc* basis, which in turn allows interest groups a diverse array of strategies for lobbying within the policy process, whether as individual firms, national organizations, or European groups targeting national or European participants in decision-making. As Padgett (1992) suggests in the case of energy policy, any major initiatives must be diluted in the quest for consensus, with the result that the most that one can hope for is for a form of 'modest incrementalism'.

A second and perhaps more serious problem of the thesis is that it simply reiterates (and Coombes is not unaware of this) the very traditional argument that organization sublimates political impulses—a point made central in Weber's writing on bureaucracy and found also in discussions ranging from Roberto Michels (1911) through Sheldon Wolin (1960), but for an alternative perspective see Goodsell (1994). There is nothing wrong with this traditional argument—it may well be accurate. It does, however, fail to take account of the distinctive context of the European Union civil service. In identifying the EU bureaucracy with the forces of routine and inertia, it becomes broadly similar to any national bureaucracy. We can develop a more refined version of the Coombes thesis, and one that says somewhat more about the impact of the EU bureaucracy than bureaucracy in general, if we think more specifically about the distinctive environment in which the EU civil service operates.

4. FORMS OF BUREAUCRATIC ACTIVITY IN THE EUROPEAN UNION

The character of a civil service is shaped to a significant degree by the constitutional environment in which it operates. For example, the constitutional environment of the United States is one of the prime explanations for the fact that the US executive, including the civil service, is a 'government of strangers' searching for support (Heclo 1977). Conversely, the 'village community' which Heclo and Wildavsky (1981) saw at the core of British government or the dominance of the Grandes Écoles trained officials of the French *corps* would be inconceivable without a system of government in which executive power is (French semi-presidentialism notwithstanding) concentrated. In each of these countries the political traditions, say, of the spoils system in the United States, the humanities educated member of the petty gentry as public servant in Britain, the militaristic element in *corps* training and organization in France, contribute to each of the four components of bureaucratic character (cohesion, caste-character, permeability, and nature of political control). But traditions and the impact of constitutions are not immutable; civil services are modified in both intended and unintended ways by the actions of governments or legislators, from the French Revolution's creation of the École Polytechnique, through the British Northcote–Trevelyan reforms of the nineteenth century, the 1884 Pendleton Act in the United States, to the market-oriented reforms of the present (see Wright 1994).

Moving on to the distinctive features of the constitution of Europe, as far as the European civil service is concerned there are three major points of importance. First, the bureaucracy is not headed by a figure with direct political legitimacy based on public election. Certainly in a number of member states it is common to have non-parliamentarians as ministers. But this is becoming less common, and in addition the 'second-hand' political authority of such figures is arguably more immediate, since they can be dismissed by an elected politician and they serve in a government in which elected politicians predominate. Second, the civil service in the guise of the Commission is given the unique constitutional responsibility to initiate legislation. It is not simply an institution for the administration of decisions taken elsewhere—the constitutional theory, if not the practice, behind most civil-service systems. Third, unlike most European political systems (but similar to the US system—see Ch. 1) there is no fusion of legislative and executive authority. As has been raised at several points throughout this study, authority in the European Union is fragmented. I have not included the common observation (see, for example, Docksey and Williams 1994) that the EU is a civil service with minimal direct service-provision responsibilities. The EU's distinction in this respect is a matter of degree rather than a major qualitative difference; ministries in many member states rely on regional or local governments to implement legislation; Swedish ministries traditionally have little direct authority over administrative boards and agencies; and the Swedish model itself has been emulated in Denmark and Britain, for example, through the creation of agencies to fulfil functions formerly carried out by ministries (see Wright 1994).

The Commission has been given a political role, as Coombes and others have suggested. But it has a political role in two rather distinct senses: in terms of its need to mobilize support and persuade other institutions and groups, and in terms of its constitutional function as an initiator of EU policy. These two rather different civil-service roles interact with more traditional conceptions of bureaucracy in a somewhat more complex manner than the simple politics–bureaucracy dichotomy that has dominated the discussion of the EU bureaucracy since Coombes.

One may broadly summarize Coombes as showing that the EU civil service has two important roles, and not only in terms of integration: implementation and initiative. In the study of public policy the terms 'implementation' and 'innovation' are certainly contentious. Where the policy process is a seamless web, the notion of implementation becomes problematic—key 'policy' decisions which shape public policies take place as policies are delivered (Hogwood and Gunn 1984). Moreover, the adage that there is nothing new under the sun has been shown to be a sound assumption when it comes to evaluating policy initiatives, and thus policies can generally best be classified as being more or less a direct continuation of what went before (Hogwood and Peters 1983). Nevertheless, the EU Commission has been given a role in initiation that is constitutionally defined rather than set in terms that would settle academic disputes about the meaning of such key policy terms—it has to recommend legislation.

Thus the European civil service, through the constitutional role of the Commission, plays an important part in initiating EU legislation as well as administering EU policies. Moreover, as was discussed above, it must operate in two distinctive arenas: the bureaucratic and the intergovernmental-interinstitutional. In both the arenas in which it operates and the roles it fulfils, the EU may not be unique when compared with member states. In many European states civil services also operate in worlds similar to the intergovernmental-interinstitutional, in so far as, say, the top three or so levels of a ministerial hierarchy are involved in the political process of securing support for a particular policy. Moreover, we all know that 'policy' and 'administration' can never be separated from each other, and that civil servants initiate and shape policy. One might suggest two distinctive features of the EU in this respect. First, the worlds of bureaucracy and intergovernmentalism (or hierarchical and co-ordinate officialdom), as well as the roles of implementer and initiator, are even less distinctly delineated by rank and position than in national bureaucracies. The top ranks of permanent officials in national bureaucracies are seldom specialists, having instead general academic qualifications not directly related to the technical aspects of their organizations, although this is not to suggest that they lack qualifications for the position. Second, while civil services everywhere have political power and are closely involved in the formulation and even the initiation of legislation, policy initiation in the EU is not merely an inevitable consequence of a permanent and technically trained or experienced administrative staff, but a *constitutional obligation*. As such, the Commission can and should take a stand on controversial issues. It can even create controversy in the first place, by proposing initiatives when no legislation exists. The constitutional role of the Commission gives the organization a legitimacy in political controversies rarely given to the permanent administrative organizations of nation states—the legitimate authority to be a major independent actor, and an initiating body, in the policy process.

The distinctiveness of the EU in the applicability of the worlds in which bureaucrats operate and the roles they fulfil is not at issue here, as the analysis in this book does not stand or fall on the uniqueness of the EU. Rather, here I am suggesting that better understanding of the impact of the main characteristics of the EU bureaucracy upon policy-making is gained if instead of looking at the rather two-dimensional politics versus administration distinction, which somewhat misleadingly sees the Commission as a hierarchical bureaucracy acting as a drag on political innovation, we look at the rather diverse roles that the Commission bureaucracy finds itself filling. Damaška's (1986) drawing attention to the interaction between different types of officialdom and roles of government helps our understanding of the role of the EU civil service, although here his concern with the nature of legal procedures means we must be careful when looking for direct parallels.[1] We may adapt Damaška's fourfold typology, combining the two different forms of officialdom (hierarchical and co-ordinate) and two different types of role (activist versus reactive state), to give four main types of activity involved in a politico-administrative system (Table 7.1). Civil servants may have an active or reactive role and operate within a bureaucratic or intergovernmental-interinstitutional world. While the coexistence of such activities may not be unique to the EU, the operation of the EU at least makes their coexistence far more obvious and striking than the process of decision-making in member states.

The traditional form of activity associated with 'classical' bureaucracies is that of *routine administration*; obeying orders, following instructions, enforcing regulations; reacting to events and changes in the world outside on the basis of written rules. This does not rule out discretion in applying the rules—officials are not the *Paragraphenautomat* who apply general principles and come up with an unambiguous answer

[1] I have avoided use of Damaška's own terms of 'policy-implementing' and 'conflict-solving' since their application in this context (with policy-implementing referring to an active state and conflict-solving to a reactive state) would conflict with the terminology used in this book. 'Implementation' in political science is generally, Pressman and Wildavsky (1984) notwithstanding, associated with more routine sets of activities involving carrying out decisions already taken. Damaška (1986: 11–12) understands the term as deriving from a particular view 'about the role of government'. It applies where 'government is conceived as a manager' rather than an agent for 'conflict resolution'. In the latter, the role of government is merely to maintain 'the social equilibrium'.

TABLE 7.1. *Categories of bureaucratic activity*

Arena	Role	
	Active	Reactive
Bureaucratic	Bureaucratic entrepreneurship	Routine administration
Intergovernmental-interinstitutional	Traditional politics	Political adjudication

—but it does stress procedure and technical expertise as a way of resolving issues. Nor does it mean that bureaucrats are only involved in routine administration. *Traditional politics*, mobilizing support and persuading people in a political environment where hierarchy cannot guarantee authority, is not simply the preserve of the politician; bureaucrats also participate in this world, albeit without the electoral political authority of the politician—a point to which we shall return. Notwithstanding the overlap between 'politics' and 'administration', the two cells 'routine administration' and 'traditional politics' have dominated the concerns of comparative students of administration. And of course this has a major justification since it raises, among other things, the central question of the involvement of bureaucrats and bureaucratic procedures in the shaping of major policy areas. But they are not the only forms of activity which involve the interaction between bureaucrats and politicians.

Bureaucratic entrepreneurship refers to the activity of officials playing a major role in policy initiation within a bureaucratic arena. This means seeking to gain the support of the organization—the directorate, the directorate general, or the Commission as a collectivity, depending on the nature of the initiative—for a policy innovation. Given the technical quality of much EU legislation, including much that has to be approved by the Council, bureaucratic entrepreneurship is the way in which technically qualified or experienced officials charged with initiating legislation set about fulfilling this constitutional obligation. *Political adjudication* refers to the reactive decisions that have to be made by the Commission as implementers of policy but within a context where intergovernmental-interinstitutional negotiation as well as, possibly even more than, technical criteria shape the decision. Thus decisions to allow state funding for ailing industries, to take member-state governments to court, or to allow or withhold a grant can be intensely political decisions, albeit ostensibly guided by general if not technical principles.

Such types of activity are analytical constructs and reality invariably mixes types. Passage of detailed regulations giving force to Council decisions involves innovation but also, in terms of the legal procedures for their ratification, may appear to be implementation. Nevertheless, if we keep these analytical categories, they allow us to examine the impact of the characteristics of the bureaucracy of the European Union in a somewhat more specific manner than is offered by the simple politics–administration distinction. Each of the types of activity has strains shaped in part by the specific character of the European Union. Let us look at each in turn.

4a. Routine administration

This form of activity is familiar as the 'classical' form of bureaucracy. Officials simply obey rules: 'hierarchical officials are prepared to live by the rigidities of a narrow [reactive] role mandated by laissez-faire ideology. Nor can they escape their narrow role—when this seems desirable to them—by exercising "inherent" discretionary rules. What they can and cannot do in the hierarchical apparatus is determined by relatively unyielding rules' (Damaška 1986: 206). A frequently raised tension in this form of activity is that between the necessarily clear formal written rules required for pure 'routine' administration (i.e. where the rules are sufficiently comprehensive and unambiguous as to allow no official any substantial discretion in the performance of his or her duties) and the empirical reality of patchy and frequently vague rules. As Hood (1976) shows, the conditions of 'perfect administration' mean that the notion of a hierarchy as a machine that converts clear instructions into a set of predicted outcomes is simply an analytical construct with few, if any, empirical referents. Thus lower grades within any organization must exercise discretion. While this has generally been discussed in the context of the 'street level bureaucrats' (Lipsky 1979), in this context we must not forget that those on the higher floors also make key policy decisions. One of the major gaps in our knowledge of policy-making in nation states as well as the European Union is of the procedures and issues involved in the passage of the apparently routine and technical laws that generally miss direct parliamentary scrutiny and yet grossly outnumber legislative acts. Such a discussion of less spectacular aspects of public policy would probably focus attention on sets of officials somewhat below the top two or three layers.

Nevertheless, the available evidence suggests that this tension and the consequent discretionary power of lower level officials is no less in the European Union than in member states. Hay (1989: 28) suggests that specific conditions within the Commission, including the fact that senior officials are frequently away from their desks, gives junior officials greater policy responsibilities than might be expected in member states. However, it is impossible to substantiate any such claim about relative power of officials at equivalent ranks in the absence of any common metric. This claim is, however, supported by somewhat more anecdotal evidence. Antonio Quatraro, the DG VI official who fell to his death from the roof of his office building in spring 1993 was an adviser—a position equivalent to that of Head of Unit and usually appointed at A3 level. This official had wide responsibilities for tobacco and potatoes and appeared to have used his position to allow organized crime easier access to the £1 billion budget allocated to the tobacco subsidy (see *Observer*, 4 April 1993). The fact that he was under investigation prior to his apparent suicide shows that the EU has means of combating corruption, yet the case offers a striking if unusual example of a widely accepted argument that officials several rungs down in the EU hierarchy have substantial discretion in the routine administration of major aspects of EU policy.

The power of the bureaucracy in routine administration derives from two features of hierarchical models of bureaucracy: the professional expertise of officials and the exclusivity of the bureaucratic process. In the EU there are, however, two important and distinctive limitations on the degree to which permanent officials can exert power through their professionalism and the degree to which outsiders can be excluded. First, the EU officials do not have a monopoly or even a plausible claim to the monopoly of expertise on which such professional power may be based. As has already been discussed, there are acknowledged shortages of 'experts' which mean that these posts have to be filled by temporary and seconded officials. Moreover, for each specialist in Brussels there are in most cases at least fifteen in the member states, as we shall discuss further below. There are substantial shortages of expertise in some areas. As already noted, Padgett (1992) discusses how the Competition directorate is handicapped by a shortage of specialists in energy and was especially dependent upon the expertise of interest groups.

Second, and possibly more important, a variety of mechanisms serve to prevent the Commission's bureaucracy from exercising important discretion through an exclusive control over issues of routine administration—decisions cannot be monopolized or even dominated by the professionals within the EU hierarchy. First, there is the sheer size of the Commission. With twenty commissioners, each with eight members of a *cabinet*, there are generally more officials within the *cabinet* than Directors within the Directorate General. Thus, as Ross (1995: 161) suggests, commissioners were in the Delors period

> more or less capable of giving effective political leadership. . . . Cabinets meddled too much in the services' business. Sometimes skilful cabinets became 'shadow cabinets' for their Commissioners' administrations, undercutting the autonomy of the appointed leaders of the Directorates General. Cabinet members, including the most junior of them, often reworked and rewrote the work of the services—sometimes 'just for the fun of it' in the words of Assistant Secretary-General Carlo Trojan.

There were a couple of spectacular cases of *cabinet* humiliation of the Director General. Commissioner Manuel Marín's clash with his Director General, Dieter Frisch, led to Frisch's resignation. Marín

> made a habit of bypassing his top officials and routinely omitted to consult Frisch on important decisions. He removed from Frisch the authority to approve all major contracts and transferred it to himself. He even issued a written instruction at one point—the breach of which can lead to immediate dismissal—that no DG VIII desk officers were to have direct contact with a particular government with which Marín was in dispute (*Observer*, 18 March 1993).

Sigismundo Crespo, a Director General in DG V who also resigned, had a similar but possibly even more humiliating experience, although unlike Frisch he was not an experienced bureaucrat. His understanding of English was limited.

> Every Monday there was a meeting between [Commissioner Padraig] Flynn and his personal staff, who formed a sort of Celtic Mafia, with names such as Tom O'Dwyer, David O'Sullivan and Hywel Jones. The immensely tall Flynn would orate at length in a thick County Mayo brogue and would then break off to say 'And what do you think Sigismundo?' (*Observer*, 16 May 1993).

Director Generals as well as Directors are appointed not only on the basis of experience, professionalism, and competence but also on the basis of nationality and political acceptability to those involved in making the decision at the time of the appointment. As we have seen, political appointees remain long after those who were responsible for their appointment have gone. In the European Union it is possible for a commissioner to inherit a senior bureaucracy which is neither technically nor politically to his liking. Commissioners have under these circumstances been able to to have senior officials moved on, although this has happened rarely. In December 1994 Commissioner Ioannis Paleokrassas was responsible for the removal of three German officials from senior positions in DG, although the difficulties involved in doing this are indicated by the fact that they were removed (two through internal redeployment, one taking early retirement) only two months before Commissioner Paleokrassas left office himself (*Der Spiegel*, 12 Dec. 1994). In November 1995 Commissioner Mario Monti dismissed Peter Wilmott, Director General of DG XXI, 'in the interests of the service' (*The European*, 2 November 1995). More usually, where top officials and commissioners do not get on, there is substantial scope for more direct control of the administration through the *cabinet*.

To some extent the possibility of commissioner intervention in the routine decisions of Commission officials can mean that member-state interests are represented, if Ross (1995: 571) is correct in identifying the tendency for commissioners to protect the interest of their home states. Lord Cockfield's experience suggests that the permanent representatives think that this is actually the role of the commissioner, since 'the UK Permanent Representative thought it was his function to see me before every meeting to acquaint me with his "views" on the various items on the agenda' and saw himself as 'a great deal more independent than most Commissioners' (Cockfield 1994: 110).

Even if the ability to secure the support of one's commissioners offers only limited scope for member-state influence, the setting up of formal committees to scrutinize the implementation of policy within the Commission, the *comitologie* of the European Union, creates further possibilities for officials from outside the EU service to participate in the promulgation of regulations to be passed by the Commission as giving effect to Council legislation. Such Commission legislation is, of course, deemed to be secondary, in the sense that it is passed under cover of Council legislation, yet to assume that Commission legislation is technical and raises no substantial controversy or policy issues would be mistaken, as it would be to assume that Council legislation deals with major questions of policy direction rather than technical details (see, for example, Wijckmans and Vanderelst 1995). In principle, almost all the secondary legislation (i.e. the regulations passed by the Commission) is subject to negotiation with officials from member states. As Bradley (1993: 719) argues, 'The creation of the supervisory committee system is possibly one of the most significant organic developments in the Community's institutional structures bringing the national administrations alongside the Community institutions in the process for adopting implementing provisions.'

4b. Bureaucratic entrepreneurship

The professional limitations on an autonomous and powerful role for the European civil service within routine administration are made particularly apparent when we look for a more active role of the civil service as an initiator of policies. There is an inherent tension between the hierarchical-bureaucratic conception of officialdom and the activity of innovating (suggested in Damaška 1986: 186). On the one hand, the hierarchical-bureaucratic conception of officialdom suggests an exclusive process of decision-making, dominated by the officials within the organization using their expertise and administrative positions to formulate proposals. On the other hand, innovatory proposals require some form of political support from outside the bureaucratic organization, in order to have any chance of becoming law. In the EU context, although the Commission might have the responsibility of proposing legislation, such proposals require Council approval and as such no longer remain a matter for the Commission bureaucracy, or even negotiation between the Council and the Commission, but a whole range of political actors including member-state civil servants and interest groups.

The authority of Commission civil servants in this process of bureaucratic entrepreneurship—initiating proposals that might eventually become EU law—derives in part from their constitutional status as the initiators of legislation, but also, paradoxically, from the political support of the commissioner. A strong commissioner, or an astute one, can help secure the collective support of the College of Commissioners for a controversial initiative. For example, the support of Carlos Ripa Di Meana was crucial in gaining acceptance for DG XI's position on stricter car emission standards in 1989 (Judge 1993). Thus administrative power in innovation requires, at least in the more controversial questions, political support.

A third basis of Commission civil-service power in initiation can be found in the expertise of officials. In terms of the characteristics of officials themselves, technical expertise is sought even among many of the top 'political' officials. In fact, those who are appointed to a directorship are not necessarily 'lay' officials with no experience. Nevertheless, technically qualified experts are more likely to be found at least two grades below that of Director. Even so, there are acknowledged wide gaps in the expertise of the EU civil service—and there are plenty of organizations with a claim to be able to fill that gap. A vivid illustration of how such gaps can lead to a relative weakening of the role of the Commission comes from attempts by the Commission to compile a list of hazardous wastes in 1994, following the 1991 Hazardous Wastes Directive:

> The Commission made valiant efforts to produce the definitive hazardous waste list required by the 1991 Directive. Each time the Commission staffers located a draft, they were inundated with criticisms that this or that waste was incorrectly listed. After numerous attempts, the Commission concluded that it was impractical for a couple of Brussels-based bureaucrats to list accurately and definitively all hazardous wastes in the EU (Hunter 1995: 85).

The criticisms came, above all, from member-state pollution experts who were able to show, for example, that the list included materials posing no known hazards and excluded some exceptionally hazardous wastes. In consequence, 'under the German Council Presidency's leadership, national bureaucrats hurriedly proposed their own hazardous wastes list, based on an earlier Franco-German proposal presented to the technical committee' (Hunter 1995: 86), and this was broadly accepted despite its flaws.

Thus despite the importance attached to the role of the Commission as an initiator of European public policies, there are substantial limitations to the specific civil-service role in it. There is little scope in this respect for Commission civil servants to act independently without mobilizing support of a commissioner (either directly or indirectly through the *cabinet*)—where Council approval is required for legislation such political support is essential. Even where Council approval is not essential, the *comitologie* structures (see above) can bring an issue into the intergovernmental-interinstitutional bargaining arena.

4c. Political adjudication

In the application of apparently technical criteria to highly politically significant legal issues, one can see the close coexistence of the bureaucratic and intergovernmental-interinstitutional worlds since there are no pure forms of political adjudication unconstrained by legal and bureaucratic rules. The notion that it is the intergovernmental-interinstitutional arena that decides how EU law is to be applied, as opposed to the hierarchical, of course, is itself a controversial issue since it implies the subversion of an impartial legal order by a partial political order. Maitland-Walker (1991), for example, complains of the 'unacceptable face of politics' in EU competition cases. Nevertheless such political adjudication is an important part of the Commission's role. This point is graphically illustrated by the fact that competition cases were routinely scrutinized, under Delors's presidency, by a member of Delors's *cabinet*, Lodewijk Briet, with problems to be raised at meetings between *chefs de cabinet*, where he represented Delors's view. As Ross (1995: 130) describes it:

> Every week hundreds, sometimes thousands of cases crossed his [Lodewijk Briet's] desk. Most were routine, but there were always a few which either bore potential legal problems or which brushed the interests of member state governments. . . . Lodewijk described Commission competition policy as part jurisprudence and part political realism. Sir Leon Brittan [commissioner responsible for competition policy in DG IV] and his staff of committed smart lawyers were always attempting to push Commission competition policy as far and as fast as they could. Other Commissioners and their staffs, including the Delors team, sometimes disagreed with this and had also to try to protect their national interests. Fighting over competition policy was thus endemic.

One might expect that the proliferation of rules, some of them provoked by apparently inconsistent and partial decisions, governing how the Commission should decide in important competition cases, would eliminate political adjudication, although it seems to survive.

In merger cases Hansen (1993) goes through the vast array of possible criteria the Commission may use in determining the permissibility of mergers, and it is never clear which ones will weigh heavier. Siragusa similarly concludes that,

> with respect to the Commission's assessment of the compatibility of a concentration with the Regulation's standard of legality, the weight given by the Commission to the different criteria to be used, for example, for the definition of the relevant products and geographical markets or for the assessment of compatibility, is likely to vary from case to case, possibly depending on pressures from member states (Siragusa and Subiotto 1991: 929).

The vexed question of the permissibility of state aids also raises issues of consistency and the protection of national interests (see Soames and

Ryan 1995). Fining infringements of EU law similarly seems to involve intergovernmental issues: a review of the Commission's actual practice shows that an effort is generally made by the Commission to relate the fine to the particular circumstances and responsibility of each participant in the infringement, but that the Commission has at times been unable to maintain a coherent fining policy between different decisions involving similar infringements (van Bael 1995: 238). Van Bael goes on to cite the contemporaneous cases of Fiat and Alpha Romeo who both got off without a fine for the same infringement for which Leyland was fined, and concludes with the suggestion, indirectly made through quoting the head of the German cartel office, that political pressures are significant in such decisions (van Bael 1995: 243). In part this is due to the design of the decision-making process in such cases: as Haslan-Jones (1995) points out in his comparative study of European antitrust regulation, the EU model of decision-making is 'ministerial' (i.e. the final decision is taken by a minister or ministerial body—a characteristic shared by the EU, Dutch, and UK systems of antitrust regulation). The procedures of regulation enforcement are at least on prima-facie grounds given an intergovernmental dimension by the fact that initiation of proceedings is taken after consultation with the Advisory Committee on Restrictive Practices and Dominant Positions, a body composed of officials from member-state civil services.

4d. Political leadership

Perhaps the most detailed description of the exercise of political leadership within the European Union—the mobilization of intergovernmental support for major political initiatives—is found from Ross's remarkable account of the Delors period of the late 1980s. This shows the very great importance of the mobilization of the bureaucracy to the exercise of political leadership in Brussels. Although Delors himself had already had a successful political career by the time he arrived in Brussels and, as Drake (1995) suggests, was widely believed to be a strong candidate for the Presidency of France, his political leadership contained a strongly bureaucratic element. His ideas and vision 'would have not been enough without great skills at mobilizing the Commission itself, for the Commission has always been his organizational base' (Ross 1995: 244). Delors's strategy, as Ross notes, was a 'version of the Monnet method': 'engineering spillovers'—a manœuvring of participants into agreements which limited the chances of resisting further moves towards the Delors vision of closer integration—and stirring up public opinion in his favour. Public mobilization of support across Europe is difficult for an appointed official known only in one country. Delors used his Commission position to increase public visibility and it is likely that this played an important part in his development of the Commission Presidency beyond that which was believed possible.

However, crucial to Delors's leadership within the Commission was his *cabinet*, of whom the most prominent members—Lamy, Lamoureux, Leygues, Dixon, Briet—were either EU or French civil servants. Ross suggests that the dominance of Delors within the Commission was derived partly from the reflected glory that continued innovation and success brought to the Commission as a whole. The strength of Delors within the College of Commissioners buttressed the power of those members of his *cabinet* who could ask for things in his name; official hierarchical channels could be circumvented and the *cabinet* could have a direct influence over what went on in other commissioners' *cabinets* and services.

> Even when cabinet actions breaking through chains of command were received negatively, they had to be tolerated because utlimate success enhanced the reputations of those who had been manipulated. If the product was recognized as good, only the President's cabinet would know how much of its quality was due to its own work. In practice, the competence and clout of the Delors cabinet had consistently been high enough that anticipating the accolades of policy success became an important reason for the victims to accept their fate (Ross 1995: 76).

Unprecedented though the success of this strategy may have been, bureaucratic statesmanship of the sort exercised by Delors was ultimately limited by the 'absence of mobilized, democratic public commitment' (Ross 195: 244), as Council eventually failed to take the decisions needed for further progress towards Delors's vision of an integrated Europe.

5. DIFFUSE POLITICAL SUPERVISION

The bureaucratic and intergovernmental-interinstitutional worlds are very closely linked in the European Union. Political leadership has a strong organizational and bureaucratic element to it. Political adjudication, raising as it does the conflict with the principle of impartial application of legal rules, is becoming increasingly surrounded by (if not actually subjected to) sets of formal rules. Bureaucratic entrepreneurship requires the mobilization of support among member states and their representatives. Even routine administration can raise issues that can be brought into the intergovernmental arena through a series of advisory committees as well as statutory *comitologie* committees. If we look at the different forms of activity of the EU civil service we can see that the corollary of its distinctive character is the distinctive character of political control over it.

If we take those areas that are presumed to be the preserve of the bureaucracy—routine administration and the promulgation of minor legislation—the role of the the EU civil service is limited by a rather distinctive form of what may be termed *diffuse political supervision.* This form of supervision does not lie solely in the fact that commissioners and possibly other senior officials within the Commission are 'political' appointees. Nor is this form of supervision particularly obtrusive in the sense that European civil servants have their superiors looking over their shoulders or issuing direct instructions to them. Diffuse political supervision contrasts with the more limited and predictable forms of political supervision which predominate in member states. The notion of ministerial responsibility which applies in almost all member states might suggest that elected ministers exercise political leadership in more innovatory and controversial policy choices. The reverse of this is that for the more humdrum and less overtly controversial aspects of government activity much is delegated, by design or default, to the civil service. The civil service, in its turn, may be more (as is commonly believed to be the case in Germany) or less (as is commonly believed to be the case in France) receptive to interest-group pressure, but it is clearly at the heart of the decision-making process. Richard Rose aptly terms legislation that results from this less spectacular policy-making process in Britain part of the 'ongoing Whitehall process' (Rose 1984). The results of the 'ongoing process' are not devoid of political controversies, but overwhelmingly such controversies involve relatively narrow ranges of interests and somewhat specialized issues. For the most part this means that the policy-making process is largely confined to a 'policy community', a set of groups, possibly also individual experts, and civil servants responsible for the particular area of activity with relatively little and infrequent direct intervention from a minister. In such communities civil servants have a pivotal role in acting for the minister, as well as acting as 'the crucial channel through which most of the other pressures must eventually be canalised' (Crowther-Hunt quoted in Jordan and Richardson 1987: 178). As Jordan and Richardson (1987: 178–9) put it: 'If policy making and its implementation takes place via networks of relationships, as we suggest, then there is little doubt that civil servants sit at the centre of the network—sometimes orchestrating and sometimes reflecting "community politics" both within and outside Whitehall.' Political control in this process is exercised in two separate ways. The first and most important, if somewhat intangible, is through the anticipated reactions civil servants have towards their minister and their government. Effective civil servants have to have some idea, when bargaining with interests and drafting legislation, of what their minister or their government would support, how far they would want their officials to push it, and how far they would be prepared to antagonize those who turn out to be opposed to it. The second form of political control may be exercised when this first form breaks down—a minister has the authority to intervene directly in the process. Within these substantial constraints, the 'policy communities' model as it is characterized in many member states gives the civil servants a high degree of autonomy in the policy process, with political controversies that spill out of the communities settled by appeal to the minister or the governing party or parties.[2]

In the European Union there exists, of course, the same form of political supervision implied by the doctrine of ministerial responsibility, made all the more effective by the relatively small number of senior permanent officials in relation to the Commissioner's own entourage, above all the *cabinet*. Yet in addition to this, a variety of mechanisms exist by which decision-making can be taken out of the bureaucratic arena (in which Commission civil servants have a pivotal role in representing the authority of the commissioner as well as acting as a channel for group interests) and placed in a much wider arena where its role is far less dominant. Groups and national civil servants both have the possibility of making controversial issues intergovernmental issues. In the case of conflict over Commission regulation, even when Council approval is not required, the *comitologie* procedure also allows these aspects of Commission activity to be subject to intergovernmental-interinstitutional bargaining. The prominent role of bureaucracy in national policy communities depends to a large extent upon the fact that

[2] Courts are, of course, an arena of growing importance in this respect. However, they are not discussed here since we are primarily concerned with the formulation of draft legislation where courts generally have little direct ability to intervene.

the participants in the decision-making process are aware of the fact that a bargain has to be struck within the bureaucratic arena and generally seek to get the best deal they can out of the civil servants with whom they interact. In the European Union, participants can appeal for help in supporting their view (or opposing that of others) to the relevant commissioner for the service. Yet they can also appeal to the commissioner from their country (if they happen to represent nation-specific interests), to representatives of particular member states, whether permanent representatives, civil servants who participate in the decision-making process in Brussels, or MPs or ministers. Issues can be taken out of the bureaucratic and into the intergovernmental-interinstitutional bargaining arena far more easily in the European Union than they can be moved out of the bureaucratic arena in most member states. In the EU this means shifting issues out of the arena in which the Commission bureaucracy can expect to play a pivotal role, into one where its role is far less certain.

Thus diffuse political supervision means that the role of the European Union civil service in decision-making is far weaker than one would expect in a member state such as Britain, France, or Germany. Issues can be taken out of a bureaucratic arena where their expertise, experience, and hands on power places EU officials in a prominent role, and moved to the political arena of intergovernmental-interinstitutional bargaining where they become one set of voices among many. This does not mean political control, since this term implies a particular instance, whether this is a body or an individual, exercising control. In fact, the diffuse political supervision system of the EU implies, although there is no means of measuring this, that the political control exercised by the minister through civil servants anticipating reactions of the minister, or rather in this case the commissioner, is weakened, since it is unclear whose reactions a civil servant should seek to anticipate—those of the commissioner, the College of Commissioners, or the Council, or perhaps those of people in another EU institution.

The argument that the European civil service represents bureaucratic ballast—a force for inertia and timid action which reduces the scope for political initiative—is also wide of the mark. The bureaucratic character of political leadership in the EU, even under Delors, is more a result of the fact that the European executive has no direct electoral legitimacy. Leadership of the ambitious sort that Delors on the whole successfully exercised was to a large extent the result of mobilizing the support of those who agreed with him, persuading those who could be persuaded, and outmanœuvring those who could not, using a bureaucratic power base because there was no other. Dominance over the agenda of the Commission, through a team of extremely adept bureaucratic politicians around Delors, was crucial to the success of his strategy. In fact, it is just as plausible to argue that, without the institutional focus of the Commission and its bureaucracy, political leadership would be impossible, whether this refers to leadership of the grander variety advocated by Coombes or to the more modest form of seeking to take the initiative in a controversial functional policy area. Without the administrative assistance of a European bureaucracy, without its experience and memory of what has been tried, what needs to be done, what has failed, and what has worked, it is difficult to imagine that any commissioner could generate a set of policy objectives let alone set about achieving them. Perhaps even more important (but less widely acknowledged), without the legitimacy and status that derives from heading an administrative organization responsible for a large and increasing portion of public policy throughout Europe, it is difficult to see on what basis commissioners could claim to have any legitimacy distinct from that given second-hand by those who appointed them.

This perception of the constraints on the EU bureaucracy presents a diagnosis somewhat different from that of the Eurosceptic seeking to take power out of the hands of an overmighty Brussels administrative machine, as well as from that of the reformer seeking to give greater powers to a European Parliament, or even national parliaments, as a way of limiting the 'democratic deficit'. If there is a problem of bureaucracy in Brussels having a greater influence on policy-making than is generally accepted in member states and thus subverting the democratic process, then this is less a consequence of the power of the EU civil service itself than of the intricate and busy world of statutory, advisory, and *ad hoc* forums of which EU civil servants are but a part. The problem of identifying responsibility and generating accountability results more from the need to mobilize support from representatives of member states in diverse, but predominantly bureaucratic, arenas of decision-making. While it is not possible for EU policies in reality 'to emerge from nowhere', as Mazey and Richardson (quoted in McLaughlin and Jordan 1993: 129–30) put it, the fact that they may appear to underlines the special difficulties of identifying responsibility in Brussels.

Some conceive of the problems of democracy in the EU policy-making process in much the same way as one might advocate democratic reform in an authoritarian state. There is a 'democratic deficit' that can be filled by giving elected representatives a greater role in the policy-making process, although the mechanisms for achieving this differ from author to author. However, such a prescription could be overlooking fundamental differences between a nation state, even a federal one, and the emerging European Union. Features of intergovernmentalism are ubiquitous in the EU political system, whether in the *comitologie* committees or the nation-state role in civil-service recruitment. Bringing more players into the system, whether through a stronger role for the European Parliament or national or regional legislatures and, perhaps even more importantly, their staffs, might not reduce the democratic deficit. Increasing the range of interests and bodies that have to be squared might increase the difficulty of identifying accountability, turning a democratic deficit into a less democratic surfeit of institutions, groups, and individuals, all with some sort of valid claim to represent European citizens.

REFERENCES

Abeles, M., I. Bellier, and M. McDonald (1993). *Approche anthropologique de la commission européenne: Executive Summary.* Brussels, European Commission.

Aberbach, J., R. Putnam, and B. A. Rockman (1981). *Bureaucrats and Politicians in Western Democracies.* Cambridge, Mass., Harvard University Press.

Abrahams, P., *et al.* (1993). 'Squabbles over EC Goodies Near an End', *Financial Times.* London, 25 Oct.

Allison, G. T. (1971). *Essence of Decision: Explaining the Cuban Missile Crisis.* Boston, Mass., Little Brown.

Anton, T. (1980). *Administered Politics: Elite Political Culture in Sweden.* Boston, Mass., Nijhoff.

Averyt W. F. (1975). 'Eurogroups, Clientela and the European Community', *International Organization*, 29: 949–72.

Berger, J., and R. Skærseth (1994). 'The Climate Policy of the EC: Too Hot to Handle', *Journal of Common Market Studies*, 32(1): 25–46.

Beuzard, J.-C., and G. White (1992). 'Unions and Professional Associations in the European Institutions', *L'Indépendent: Bulletin of the Association of Independent Officials for the Defence of the European Civil Service* (Sept./Oct.), 32–3.

Blondel, J. (1985). *Government Ministers in the Contemporary World.* London, Sage.

—— and J.-L. Thiebault, eds. (1991). *The Profession of Government Minister in Western Europe.* London, Macmillan.

Blumann, C. (1989). 'La Commission, agent d'execution du droit communutaire: La Comitologie', in J.-V. Louis and D. Waelbroeck (eds.), *La Commission au cœur du système institutionnel des communautés européennes.* Brussels, Institut d'Études Européennes.

Bourtembourg, C. (1987). 'La Commission des Communautés Européennes: Son personnel', in S. Cassese (ed.), *The European Administration.* Paris, International Institute of Administrative Sciences.

Bradley, K. S. C. (1993). 'Comitology and the Law: Through a Glass Darkly', *Common Market Law Review*, 28(4): 693–721.

Brittan, L. (1994). *Europe: The Europe we Need.* London, Hamish Hamilton.

Buitendijk, G. J., and M. P. C. M. van Schendelen (1995). 'Brussels Advisory Committees: A Channel for Influence', *European Law Review*, 20(1): 37–56.

Bunyan, T., ed. (1993). *Statewatching the New Europe: A Handbook on the European State*. Nottingham, Russell Press.

Butt Phillip, A. (1991). *Directory of Pressure Groups in the European Community*. London, Longman.

Caplan, J. (1988). *Government without Administration: State and Civil Service in Weimar and Nazi Germany*. Oxford, Clarendon Press.

Carvel, J. (1994). 'Kinnock Picks Eurocrat Aide', *Guardian*. Manchester, 16 Sept.

Cassese, S. (1987). 'Divided Powers: European Administration and National Administrations', in S. Cassese (ed.), *The European Administration*. Paris, International Institute of Administrative Sciences.

Chapman, B. (1959). *The Profession of Government*. London, Allen & Unwin.

Christensen, T. (1991). 'Bureaucratic Roles: Political Loyalty and Professional Autonomy', *Scandinavian Political Studies*, 14(4): 303–20.

Church, C. H., and D. Phinnemore (1994). *European Union and European Community: A Handbook and Commentary on the Post-Maastricht Treaties*. New York, Harvester Wheatsheaf.

Churchill, R. R. (1987). *EEC Fishing Law*. Dordrecht, Martinus Nijhoff.

Claude, I. L. J. (1956). *Swords into Plowshares: The Problems and Progress of International Organization*. London, University of London Press.

Clergerie, J.-L. (1995). 'L'Improbable censure de la commission européenne', *Revue du droit public*, 1995(1): 201–20.

Cockfield, L. (1994). *The European Union: Creating the Single Market*. London, Wiley.

Cohen, S. S. (1977). *Modern Capitalist Planning: The French Model*. Berkeley, University of California Press.

Coleman, W. D. (1989). 'Strong States and Weak States: Sectoral Networks in Advanced Capitalist Economies', *British Journal of Political Science*, 19(1): 47–62.

Committee on Budgets (1992). *Report of the Committee on the Budget on the Staff Policy of the Community Institutions*. Luxembourg, European Parliament Committee on the Budget.

—— (1994). *Report of the Committee on the Budget on the Staff Policy of the Community Institutions*. Luxembourg, European Parliament Committee on the Budget.

Committee on Institutional Affairs (1993). *Report of the Committee on Institutional Affairs on the Role of National Experts and the Commission's Right of Initiative*. Luxembourg, European Parliament Committee on Institutional Affairs.

Coombes, D. (1970). *Politics and Bureaucracy in the European Community: A Portrait of the Commission of the EEC*. London, Allen & Unwin.

Crozier, M. (1964). *The Bureaucratic Phenomenon*. London, Tavistock.

Damaška, M. R. (1986). *The Faces of Justice and State Authority: A Comparative Analysis of the Legal Process*. New Haven, Yale University Press.

Daussin, A. (1959). 'Vers une fonction publique européenne', *European Yearbook*, 6: 112–54.

Derlien, H.-U. (1990). 'Continuity and Change in the West German Federal Executive Élite', *European Journal of Political Research*, 18(3): 349–72.

Docksey, C., and K. Williams (1994). 'The Commission and the Execution of Community Policy', in G. Edwards and D. Spence (eds.), *The European Commission*. London, Longman.

Dogan, M. (1975). 'The Political Power of Western Mandarins', in M. Dogan (ed.), *The Manadarins of Western Europe: The Political Role of Top Civil Servants*. London and Beverly Hills, Calif., Sage.

Donnelly, M., and E. Ritchie (1994). 'The College of Commissioners and their *Cabinets*', in G. Edwards and D. Spence (eds.), *The European Commission*. London, Longman.

Drake, H. (1995). 'Political Leadership and European Integration: The Case of Jacques Delors', *West European Politics*, 18(1): 140–60.

Dubois, L. (1993). 'Renationalisation?' in J. Penaud (ed.), *La Fonction publique des communautés europćenes*. Paris, La Documentation française.

Dyson, K. (1977). 'The West German 'Party Book' Administration: An Evaluation', *Public Administration Bulletin*, 25: 3–23.

Earnshaw, D., and D. Judge (1993). 'The European Parliament and the Sweeteners Directive: From Footnote to Inter-institutional Conflict', *Journal of Common Market Studies*, 31(3): 103–16.

ECSC Treaty (1951). *Treaty Establishing the European Coal and Steel Community*. London, British Iron and Steel Confederation.

Egeberg, M. (1995). *Organization and Nationality in the European Commission Services*. Oslo, Arena Working Paper 13, Apr.

Eldersveld, S. J., J. Kooiman, and T. van der Tak (1981). *Elite Images of Dutch Politics: Accommodation and Conflict*. Ann Arbor, Mich., University of Michigan Press.

European Commission (1988). *Voici vos reponses: Résultats de l'enquête d'opinion auprès des membres du personnel réalisée par la Cegos*. Brussels, Commission of the European Communities.

—— (1993). 'Les Fonctionnaires européens: privilégiés et trop nombreux?' *Courrier du personnel*, 8(4): 1.

—— (1994*a*). *Do* You *Believe All You Read in the Newspapers*? London, Commission of the European Communities.

—— (1994*b*). *Institutions of the Community*. Background report, ISEC/B7. London, Commission of the European Communities.

—— (1994*c*). *The European Environment Agency*. Background report, ISEC/B6. London, Commission of the European Communities.

—— (1994*d*). *The European Medicine Evaluation Agency*. Background report, ISEC/B23. London, Commission of the European Communities.

—— (1995). The Community Budget: The Facts in Figures. Luxembourg, Office for Official Publications.

European Investment Bank (1994). *Annual Report 1993*. Luxembourg, European Investment Bank.

Eurosources (1994). *InstiContact 1994: Guide to Contacts in the European Institutions.* Brussels, Prometheus.

Featherstone, K. (1994). 'Jean Monnet and the Democratic Deficit in the European Union', *Journal of Common Market Studies*, 32(2): 149–70.

Fry, G. (1993). *Reforming the Civil Service*. Edinburgh, Edinburgh University Press.

George, S. (1991). *Politics and Policy in the European Community*. 2nd edn. Oxford, Oxford University Press.

Goodsell, C. T. (1994). *The Case for Bureaucracy: A Public Administration Polemic.* 3rd edn. New York, Chatham House Publishers Inc.

Gozens, M. (1992). 'Consumer Protection in the Single European Market', *Common Market Law Review*, 29(1): 71–92.

Grant, C. (1994). *Delors: Inside the House that Jack Built.* London, Nicholas Brealy Publishing.

Guardian (1994). 'The Price of Messing with Mr Kohl', *Guardian*. 31 Oct.

Hansen, M. (1993). 'Collective Dominance under EC Merger Control Regulation', *Common Market Law Review*, 30(4): 787–828.

Haslan-Jones, A. (1995). 'A Comparative Analysis of the Decision Taking Process', *European Competition Law Review*, 16(3): 154–80.

Hay, R. (1989). *The European Commission and the Administration of the Community*. Brussels, Commission of the European Communities.

Hayes-Renshaw, F., C. Lequesne, and P. M. Lopez (1989). 'The Permanent Representations of the Member States to the European Communities', *Journal of Common Market Studies*, 38(2): 119–37.

Hayward, J. E. S. (1986). *The State and the Market Economy: Industrial Patriotism and Economic Intervention in France*. Brighton, Wheatsheaf Books.

—— (1995). 'Organized Interests and Public Policies', in J. E. S. Hayward and E. C. Page (eds.), *Governing the New Europe*. Cambridge, Polity Press.

Headey, B. (1974). *British Cabinet Ministers*. London, Allen & Unwin.

Heclo, H. (1977). *A Government of Strangers*. Washington, DC, Brookings.

—— (1978). 'Issue Networks and the Executive Establishment', in A. King (ed.), *The New American Political System*. Washington, DC, American Enterprise Institute.

—— (1984). 'In Search of a Role: America's Higher Civil Service', in E. N. Suleiman, *Bureaucracy and Policy Making: A Comparative Overview*. New York, Holmes & Meier.

—— (1988). 'The In-and-outer System: A Critical Assessment', *Political Quarterly*, 10(3): 37–56.

—— and A. Wildavsky (1981). *Private Government of Public Money*. London, Macmillan.

Hennessy, P. (1989). *Whitehall*. London, Fontana.

Hine, D. (1993). *Governing Italy: The Politics of Bargained Pluralism*. Oxford, Oxford University Press.

Hintze, O. (1964*a*). 'Der Beamtenstand' (1911), in O. Hintze, *Soziologie und Geschichte: Gesammelte Abhandlungen zur Soziologie, Politik und Theorie der Geschichte*. Göttingen, Vandenhoeck & Ruprecht.

—— (1964*b*). 'Der Commissarius und seine Bedeutung in der allgemeinen Verwaltungsgeschichte', in O. Hintze, *Staat und Verfassung: Gesammelte Abhandlungen zur allgemeinen Verfassungsgechichte*. Göttingen, Vandenhoeck & Ruprecht.

Hofstede, G. (1980). *Culture's Consequences*. London and Beverly Hills, Calif., Sage.

Hogwood, B. W., and L. A. Gunn (1984). *Policy Analysis for the Real World*. Oxford, Oxford University Press.

—— and B. G. Peters (1983). *Policy Dynamics*. Brighton, Wheatsheaf Books.

Hood, C. (1976). *The Limits of Administration*. London, John Wiley.

—— and B. G. Peters (1994). 'Understanding RHPOs', in C. Hood and B. G. Peters (eds.), *Rewards at the Top: A Comparative Study of High Public Office*. London, Sage.

Hooghe, L. (1994). *Building a Europe with the Regions: The Politics of the European Commission under the Structural Funds*. Oxford, Nuffield College Centre for European Studies.

Hooper, J. (1994). 'Hopes Rise of End to Commission Row.' *Guardian*. Manchester, 11 July.

Hunter, R. (1995). 'The Problematic EU Hazardous Wastes List', *European Environmental Law Review* (March): 83–8.

Johnson, B. (1993). 'EC Job Fixing Exposed', *Daily Telegraph*. London, 17 Mar.

Jordan, A. G. (1981). 'Iron Triangles, Wooly Corporatism and Elastic Nets: Images of the Policy Process', *Journal of Public Policy*, 1(2): 95–123.

—— and J. J. Richardson (1987). *British Politics and the Policy Process*. London, Allen & Unwin.

Judge, D. (1993). '"Predestined to Save the Earth": The Environment Committee of the European Parliament', in D. Judge (ed.), *A Green Dimension for the European Community*. London, Frank Cass.

Kassim, H. (1994). 'Policy Networks, Networks and European Union Policy Making', *West European Politics*, 17(4): 15–27.

Kaufman, H. J. (1981). *The Administrative Behavior of Federal Bureau Chiefs*. Washington, DC, The Brookings Institute.

Keeler, J. (1981). 'The Corporatist Dynamic of Agricultural Modernisation in the Fifth Republic', in W. G. Andrews and S. Hoffman (eds.), *The Fifth Republic at Twenty*. Albany, NY, State University of New York Press.

Kellner, P., and L. Crowther-Hunt (1980). *The Civil Servants*. London, Futura.

Kjellberg, F. (1984). 'Policy Styles in Western Europe', *Journal of Public Policy*, 4(3): 271–3 (book review).

Kunz, J. L. (1947). 'Privileges and Immunities of International Organizations', *American Journal of International Law*, 41: 828–62.

Lane, T. (1986). *Grey Dawn Breaking*. Manchester, Manchester University Press.

LaPalombara, J. (1964). *Interest Groups in Italian Politics*. Princeton, Princeton University Press.

Lasok, D., and J. W. Bridge (1982). *An Introduction to the Law and Institutions of the European Communities*. London, Butterworths.

Lenaerts, K. (1991). 'Some Reflections on the Separation of Powers in the European Community', *Common Market Law Review*, 28(1): 11–35.

Leonard, D. (1993). 'Don Sigismundo Storms out of EC Beanfeast chez Jacques', *Observer*. London, 16 May.

Lipsky, M. (1979). *Street Level Bureaucracy*. New York, Russell Sage Foundation.

Lodge, J. (1985). 'Euro-Elections and the European Parliament: The Dilemmas Over Turnout and Powers', *Parliamentary Affairs*, 38(1): 40–56.

Lowi, T. J. (1964). 'American Business, Public Policy, Case Studies and Political Theory', *World Politics*, 16: 677–715.

—— (1969). The *End of Liberalism*. New York, Norton.

Ludlow, P. (1991). 'The European Commission', in R. O. Keohane and S. Hoffmann (eds.), *The European Community: Decisionmaking and Institutional Change*. Boulder, Colo., Westview Press.

Lynn, J., and A. Jay (1982). *Yes Minister: The Diaries of a Cabinet Minister by the Rt. Hon. James Hacker MP*. 2 vols. London, British Broacasting Corporation.

MacIntyre, D., and S. Helm (1995). 'Kohl and Chirac attack Brussels. *Independent on Sunday*. London, 17 Dec.

McLaughlin, A., and J. Greenwood (1995). 'The Management of Interest Representation in the European Union', *Journal of Common Market Studies*, 33(1): 143–56.

—— A. G. Jordan, and W. A. Maloney (1993). 'Corporate Lobbying in the European Community', *Journal of Common Market Studies*, 31(2): 191–212.

—— and A. G. Jordan (1993). 'The Rationality of Lobbying in Europe: Why are Some Euro-Groups so Numerous and so Weak? Some Evidence from the Car Industry', in S. Mazey and J. Richardson (eds.), *Lobbying in the European Community*. Oxford, Oxford University Press.

Maitland-Walker, J. (1991). 'The Unacceptable Face of Politics in Competition Cases', *European Competition Law Review*, 12(1): 3–4.

Marin, B., and R. Mayntz, eds. (1991). *Policy Networks: Empirical Evidence and Theoretical Considerations*. Frankfurt-am-Main, Campus Verlag.

Maurer, A. (1995). 'Das Europäische Parlament und das Investiturverfahren der Kommission—Bilanz eines Experiments', *Integration*, 18(2): 88–97.

Mayntz, R., and F. W. Scharpf (1975). *Policy Making in the German Federal Bureaucracy*. Amsterdam, Elsevier.

Mazey, S., and J. Richardson (1993). 'Introduction: Transference of Power, Decision Rules, and Rules of the Game', in S. Mazey and J. Richardson (eds.), *Lobbying in the European Community*. Oxford, Oxford University Press.

Merry, H. J. (1955). 'The European Coal and Steel Community—Operation of the High Authority', *Western Political Quarterly*, 8(2): 166–85.

Mezey, M. L. (1979). *Comparative Legislatures*. Durham, NC, North Carolina University Press.

—— (1995). 'Parliament in the New Europe', in J. E. S. Hayward and E. C. Page (eds.), *Governing the New Europe*. Cambridge, Polity Press.

Michels, R. (1911). *Zur Soziologie des Parteiwesens in der modernen Demokratie*. Leipzig, W. Klinkhardt.

Miers, D., and A. C. Page (1982). *Legislation*. London, Sweet & Maxwell.

Monnet, J. (1978). *Memoirs*. London, Collins.

Neisser, H. (1982). 'Die Rolle der Bürokratie im Regierungsprozeß', in H. Fischer (ed.), *Das politische System Österreichs*. Vienna, Europa Verlag.

Nettl, J. P. (1968). 'The State as a Conceptual Variable', *World Politics*, 20: 559–92.

Padgett, S. (1992). 'The Single European Energy Market: The Politics of Realization', *Journal of Common Market Studies*, 30(1): 53–75.

Page, E. C. (1992). *Political Authority and Bureaucratic Power: A Comparative Analysis*. Hemel Hempstead, Herts., Harvester Wheatsheaf.

—— (1991). 'Bureaucrats and their Brothers in Law', paper presented at the Annual Conference of the Political Studies Association, Lancaster.

—— and L. Wouters (1994*a*). 'Bureaucratic Politics and Political Leadership in Brussels', *Public Administration*, 72(3): 445–61.

—— and —— (1994*b*). 'Paying the Top People in Europe', in C. Hood and B. G. Peters (eds.), *Rewards at the Top: A Comparative Study of High Public Office*. London, Sage.

Palmer, J. (1994). 'Network of Deals around Delors Heir', *Guardian*. Manchester, 31 May.

Peeters, L. (1968). 'L'Impôt communautaire sur les rémunerations des fonctionnaires et agents des Communautés Européennes', *International Review of Administrative Sciences*, 34: 255–67.

Personnel and Administration (1992). 'Recruitment Requirements in the Community Institutions' (unpubl. paper). Brussels, European Commission DG IX.

Peters, B. G. (1981). 'The Problem of Bureaucratic Government', *Journal of Politics*, 43(1): 56–82.

—— (1992). 'Bureaucratic Politics and the Institutions of the European Community', in A. Sbragia (ed.), *Euro-Politics: Institutions and Policymaking in the 'New' European Community*. Washington DC, Brookings Institution.

Peterson, J. (1995). 'Policy-Making in the European Union: Towards a Framework for Analysis', *Journal of European Public Policy*, 2(1): 69–74.

Pressman, J. L., and A. Wildavsky (1984). *Implementation*. Berkeley, Calif., University of California Press.

Putnam, R. D. (1973). 'The Political Status of Senior Civil Servants in Western Europe: A Preliminary Analysis', *British Journal of Political Science*, 3(3): 257–90.

Ranshofen-Wertheimer, E. F. (1945). *The International Secretariat: A Great Experiment in International Administration*. Washington, DC, Carnegie Endowment for International Peace.

Rhodes, R., and D. Marsh (1992). 'Policy Networks in British Politics: A Critique of Existing Approaches', in R. A. W. Rhodes and D. Marsh (eds.), *Policy Networks in British Government*. Oxford, Clarendon Press.

Richardson, J. J., ed. (1982). *Policy Styles in Western Europe*. London, Allen & Unwin.

—— and A. G. Jordan (1979). *Governing Under Pressure*. Oxford, Martin Robertson.

Robinson, A., and C. T. Sandford (1983). *Tax Policy-Making in the United Kingdom: A Study of Rationality, Ideology and Politics*. London, Heinemann Educational Books.

Roehl, J. C. G. (1994). *The Kaiser and his Court: Wilhelm II and the Government of Germany*. Cambridge, Cambridge University Press.

Rose, R. (1980). 'Governments Against Subgovernments: A European Perspective on Washington', in R. Rose and E. N. Suleiman (eds.), *Presidents and Prime Ministers*. Washington, DC, American Enterprise Institute.

—— (1981). 'The Political Status of Higher Civil Servants in Europe', *University of Strathclyde Studies in Public Policy*, 92. Glasgow.

—— (1984). *Do Parties Make a Difference?* 2nd edn. London, Macmillan.

—— (1987). *Ministers and Ministries: A Functional Analysis*. Oxford, Clarendon Press.

Ross, G. (1995). *Jacques Delors and European Integration*. Cambridge, Polity Press.

Rotacher, A., and M. Colling (1987). 'The Community's Top Management: A Meritocracy in the Making', *Staff Courier* (Brussels), 489: 10–25.

Sbragia, A. (1992). 'Introduction', in A. Sbragia (ed.), *Euro-Politics: Institutions and Policymaking in the 'New' European Community*. Washington, DC, Brookings Institution.

Schmitt, H. A. (1962). *The Path to European Union: From the Marshall Plan to the Common Market*. Baton Rouge, La., Louisiana State University Press.

Searls, E. (1981). 'Ministerial Cabinets and Elite Theory', in J. Howarth and P. G. Cerny (eds.), *Elites in France: Origins, Reproduction and Power*. London, Frances Pinter.

Sheriff, P. (1976). 'The Sociology of Public Bureaucracies', *Current Sociology*, 24: 1–175.

Shore, C., and A. Black (1992). 'The European Communities and the Construction of Europe', *Anthropology Today*, 8(3): 10–12.

Siragusa, M., and R. Subiotto (1991). 'The EC Merger Control Regulation: The Commission's Evolving Case Law', *Common Market Law Review*, 28(4): 877–934.

Sloot, T., and P. Verschuren (1990). 'Decision Making Speed in the European Community', *Journal of Common Market Studies*, 29(1): 75–85.

Smith, M. (1992). 'The Agricultural Policy Community: Maintaining a Closed Relationship', in R. A. W. Rhodes and D. Marsh (eds.), *Policy Networks in British Government*. Oxford, Clarendon Press.

Soames, T., and A. Ryan (1995). 'State Aid and Air Transport', *European Competition Law Review*, 16(5): 290–309.

Song, Y.-H. (1995). 'The EC's Common Fisheries Policy in the 1990s', *Ocean Development and International Law*, 29(1): 31–55.

Spence, D. (1994). 'Staff and Personnel Policy in the Commission', in G. Edwards and D. Spence (eds.), *The European Commission*. London, Longman.

Spierenberg, D. (1979). *Proposals for Reform of the Commission of the European Communities and its Services*. Brussels, Commission of the European Communities.

Strasser, D. (1992). *The Finances of Europe*. Luxembourg, Office for Official Publications of the European Communities.

—— (1992). 'Les Metamorphoses du budget général des Communautés Européennes: Effets sur sa transparence', *Revue Française des Finances Publiques*, 40(2): 150–61.

Suleiman, E. N. (1975). *Politics, Power and Bureaucracy in France*. Princeton, Princeton University Press.

—— (1978). *Elites in French Society*. Princeton, Princeton University Press.

—— (1987). *Private Power and Centralization in France: The Notaires and the State*. Princeton, Princeton University Press.

Thoenig, J.-C. (1973). *L'Ère des téchnocrates*. Paris, Éditions d'Organisation.

Vallely, P. (1993). 'How Far Can We Trust Him?' *Daily Telegraph*. London, 18 Mar.

Van Bael, I. (1995). 'Fining à la Carte: The Lottery of EU Competition Law', *European Competition Law Review*, 16(4): 237–43.

Watson, R. (1995). 'Santer Buries Register of Interests', *The European*. London, 5 May.

Wealcode, S., and H. Wallace (1995). 'EC Regulation and National Enterprise', in J. E. S. Hayward (ed.), *Industrial Enterprise and European Integration*. Oxford, Oxford University Press.

Weber, M. (1972). *Wirtschaft und Gesellschaft,* 5e Aufl. Tübingen, JCB Mohr.

—— (1988). 'Parlament und Regierung im neugeordnetem Deutschland', in M. Weber, *Gesammelte Politische Schriften*. Tübingen, JCB Mohr (Paul Siebeck).

Westlake, M. (1994). 'The Commission and the Parliament', in G. Edwards and D. Spence (eds.), *The European Commission*. London, Longman.

Wijckmans, F., and A. Vanderelst (1995). 'The EC Commission's Draft Regulation on Motor Vehicle Distribution: Alea Iacta est?' *European Competition Law Review*, 16(4): 225–36.

Wilks, S. (1992). *Models of European Administration: DGIV and the Administration of Competition Policy*. European Group of Public Administration, Pisa.

—— and L. McGowan (1995). 'Disarming the Commission: The Debates over the European Cartel Office', *Journal of Common Market Studies*, 33(2): 259–74.

Willis, V. (1982). *Britons in Brussels: Officials in the European Commission and the Council Secretariat*. London, Policy Studies Institute.

Wishlade, F. (1993). 'Competition Policy, Cohesion and the Coordination of Regional Aids in the EC', *European Competition Law Review*, 14(4): 142–50.

Wolf, J. (1993). 'Industry can now look to friends within the EC', *Guardian*. 23 Jan.

Wolin, S. S. (1960). *Politics and Vision: Continuity and Innovation in Western Political Thought*. Boston, Little Brown.

Wright, V. (1994). 'Reshaping the State: The Implications for Public Administration', *West European Politics*, 17(3): 102–37.

Wynia, B. (1974). 'Federal Bureaucrats' Attitudes towards a Democratic Ideology', *Public Administration Review*, 34(2): 156–67.

Young, H., and A. Sloman (1982). *No Minister*. London, British Broadcasting Corporation.

INDEX